From Cage to Couch

~ a true story of rescue ~

Kris Wood

Nova Publishing

Bakersfield, California

Nova Publishing
http://www.NovaPublishing.org
Nova Publishing and the "*NOVA*" logo are service marks
belonging to Nova Publishing, Bakersfield, CA

This book is dedicated to my family for supporting my need to help "just one more" and all the rescuers that work tirelessly to do the work they do.

"Dogs are not our whole life, but they make our lives whole."

-Roger Caras

From Cage
to Couch

Table of Contents

Introduction

Chapter

Introduction

"Meeting our cast of characters"

Before I begin the story of our journey with Chief I would like to introduce our "cast of characters" all of whom contributed so much to the dog Chief is today.

I am Kris and I live in a small rural town in Southern California with my husband Bert. We live on a small ranch in the mountains and have been here for about seven years. I have been a teacher for twelve years and have worked at our community elementary/middle school since we moved to the area. I have been "obsessed" with horses since the age of six and have owned and competed them since the age of eighteen. I had cats all through my childhood as our household and yard did not lend itself to canine care. However, when my husband to be and I moved in together, he had had dogs all of his life and was currently being owned by a personality filled German Wirehair Pointer named Jager. That being said, I wanted one that was "ours" and had always loved Beagles. So our search began and we started our pack with our first hound, Cowboy.

Bert, my husband of seven years, is an amazing craftsman and one of those individuals who is good at just about everything he tries. We have known each other for, going on, twenty plus years and met through our love of horses. Bert has a job that is difficult to explain if you are not involved with horses, so this is the explanation in layman's terms.

Meet Chief, our newest addition to the family

He has become an amazing dog

We participate in an equestrian sport called Three Day Eventing. This sport consists of three separate portions of competition dressage, cross country jumping, and stadium jumping. Bert is involved in the second part of the competition, cross country jumping. He is responsible for building and sometimes designing the courses that make up this part of the event. He builds jumps from natural materials such as logs and brush and uses the terrain for water complexes, ditches and banks. He carves objects like ducks, whales, guns, and bulls, all from mammoth logs, for horses to jump.

These show grounds are large pieces of property where he uses large machinery to move earth from one place to another, create lakes, dig moats, and make hills and mounds where there were none. He has earned a reputation as one of the best in the industry which has allowed him to work on some of the most beautiful show grounds in the country. Acres and acres of happy hunting grounds for a pack of hounds!

The pack…Jager, Cowboy, and Indian. What a motley crew! Jager came with Bert, went with Bert, follows Bert, works with Bert…They are like bacon and eggs, Bert and Ernie, macaroni and cheese…very rarely was one without the other. I was tolerated but Jager was definitely Bert's dog. He was very bristly, growly, and could be very intimidating if you didn't know him. No one was allowed to approach Bert's truck while Jager was in it without hearing the soundtrack from "Cujo". Jager suffered from severe separation anxiety, to the point of tearing the molding off doorways, shredding curtains, ripping up carpet, and sounding as if the "hounds of hell" were coming. Because of this, he went everywhere with Bert and the truck was his second home. Now, pair this grump with a new Beagle puppy and what do you get? A bristly, grouchy, snarky, push over of a "brother". For all of his quirks, Jager was a very obedient dog. He stayed, came, sat, shook, and hung around when he was asked to. He was the perfect dog to train a new puppy.

Cowboy, or "Hotshot Cowboy" as he was registered, came from a wonderful couple out in the middle of nowhere. We were looking for a beagle that would grow up to be small enough for me to fit under a plane seat for my trips to see Bert at job sites. I wanted a tri color male and Cowboy melted my heart the moment I saw him. I know I'm biased but he was THE most perfect puppy experience one could ever hope for. He fell asleep in my arms for the long drive home, only had one accident in the house, only chewed one CD (one I didn't like anyway!), and loved Jager despite his nature.

Cowboy's young life consisted of being tied to Jager while at job sites with Bert to learn the ropes of sticking around, hunting, and coming when Dad called. He became a truck veteran and simply fell asleep on truck rides. He made two cross country trips with us and my horse to Montana and Michigan. We discovered he absolutely loves hotels! He never quite made the size requirement we had hoped for...he is a 50+ pound, mega Beagle and would never fit under a plane seat! He is an amazing hunter, snuggler, guard dog and the love of my life. My first...but not my last! Enter...Indian.

I was feeling the need to get another puppy so Cowboy would not be alone if anything should happen to Jager. Jager has been "ancient" since I've known him and he had done such a wonderful job "raising" Cowboy, I thought we should take advantage of his longevity. We ended up going back to the same couple we had gotten Cowboy from, hoping we could get a relative, same size, same temperament, same... perfection. Well, Indian, or "Bad Boy Indian" as he was registered, was a nephew of Cowboy and ended up as opposite of Cowboy as we could have gotten.

Poor Indian threw up and had to potty multiple times during the long drive home, his potty training experience was a nightmare, he chewed on everything, and would do everything he could to drive both Cowboy and Jager crazy. He is a small, feisty, "smart ass" of a dog that makes me laugh every day. His young life consisted of being tied to Jager and Cowboy for short amounts of time, before a fight would break out. He was small enough to fly with me to meet Bert in Montana one summer, where he really grew up and came into his own. He is a complete athlete, also known as the "Cheetah", a stealth hunter, and has turned into an incredible love bug, the other love of my life. However, he has been dubbed "the criminal" by many that know him.

In addition to our wonderful pack of puppies, we have been blessed with an amazing herd of horses. They all have very distinct personalities and are very talented on top of it. Mo is the beautiful, blue eyed, paint horse that, due to an accident we had, has a neurological condition that prohibits him from being ridden. He is a bit grouchy and has never been great with the dogs. He fancies himself the "top dog" of the herd and to our surprise, the others do to! Then we have my beautiful, Thoroughbred mare, Mama. She is a kind hearted girl that has helped me through some tough times, she is definitely my "rock" and I feel most confident on her. She really couldn't care less about the dogs and usually ignores them unless they are swimming in her water bucket or trying to eat her grain. Homes or Homer is our very laid back, big, Thoroughbred gelding. He loves the dogs and will sometimes blow in their fur or accept licks on the nose. He will even share carrots with Cowboy. Finally, there is Norman who is the only red head of the group. He is the only one who actually grew up on our property and he and Indian became close friends. They have even been caught playing together. All of the horses are very good around the dogs and we go out on our local trails together as often as we can. Great exercise and stress relief for all involved.

These are all of the characters, and when I say "characters", I really mean it, that have been responsible for forming the lab rat that Chief was when he got here into the amazing dog that he has become. Each one played an important role in bringing out what was buried so deeply in him to create a fantastic, resilient, and trusting member of our family.

Chapter 1

Not Another One

"We don't need another dog," my husband said, "the last thing I want to do is cart four dogs around in the truck!"

Well, that was how our story started.

I first heard about the 40 laboratory Beagles that had been rescued from the abuse of years of useless medical testing in Spain from my mom, right around Thanksgiving. She had heard the heartbreaking, yet inspiring story on the news one evening and told me about them. Being a diehard fan of the two Beagles we already own, of course, my first thought was to adopt one right away. But, as usual, we all were sidetracked by our everyday lives and the idea was gone...but not forgotten.

A week or so later, I was meeting with my colleges on a day off from school, going over lesson plans and curriculum. We were on a roll. My new birthday laptop brought me, a bit unwillingly, into the technological present, and we were working away. In the midst of creating lessons and planning the rest of the year, I received an email from my sister, also an avid animal lover. I was so excited that the computer was working and that I was getting email somewhere other than my old rickety computer cabinet in my office at home, that I opened it right away, not knowing what I was about to see.

I didn't even get the video started. When I realized it was footage of seven rescue Beagles' first time out of their crates...I knew I would cry. Just seeing the still shot of their scared, thin little faces through the crate doors made me tear up. It would have to wait until I was alone and could blubber in the comfort of my own home, surrounded by my own Beagles.

And blubber I did. The images of these poor, adorable, Beagles afraid to come out of their crates was too much. I cried and cried watching the first then another and another Beagle emerge from their little caves onto the grass FOR THE FIRST TIME! I was enraged at the same time that these amazing dogs are used for experiments. I thought about how wonderful my two Beagles, Cowboy and Indian, are and all the things they get to experience every day. Looking at them curled up on the couch, I was sitting on the floor, as usual, and all their toys (most of them just skins at this point) spread out all over the house my disbelief and disgust just increased as did the volume of tears I shed for these poor little guys.

That was it! My campaign to convince my husband, Bert, that we needed to step up and rescue a laboratory Beagle from Spain, had begun!

Chapter 2

My Plan

After hugging Cowboy (Cows for short) and Indian (Shmin for …) until they both thought I was crazy, I decided to text Bert in Montana. He was there with Jay, his associate, for a three week stay working on some major changes at a job site.

My husband builds cross country courses for Equestrian 3 Day Event competitions. He travels frequently and luckily during the summers we pack up the dogs and sometimes the horses and head off to Montana. It is one of the most beautiful equestrian facilities there is and the most wonderful place for the dogs to run, swim, well, basically, just be dogs. Cowboy, Indian, and Jager (the ancient bird dog) have been visiting for years now. Bert also builds many local shows where the dogs are well known and have free run of acres upon acres of prime hunting and playing property.

Well, it was ten o'clock at home so it would be eleven o'clock in Montana…he would probably already be asleep, but I had to try! I sent him the text that simply said, "Can we please - please – please - please adopt a Beagle from Spain?" I pressed send and waited.

The next morning I still hadn't gotten a response, which isn't unusual; luckily I had another reason to get a hold of him…frozen pipes this morning, no water! He responded quickly to that one! I had to ask him if he got the other text while I had his texting attention. The response I got confused me…"yes". Yes to what, I wondered. Yes to he got the text message, or yes we can adopt a Beagle. I had to get going to school, but I just couldn't let this go, it was going to drive me crazy all day!

I teach middle school Science at our local school. It has been a very difficult year…so anything positive that could have possibly happened was welcomed and pursued! I am lucky enough to have a preparation period to start my day. I took this time to text Bert again to get clarification and perhaps conformation on my Beagle adoption plan. My message said exactly what I was wondering…"Yes you got my message or yes we can get a Beagle?" Seemed like an easy question to me! I waited but time didn't stop so I had to get to work. I checked my phone after every period and finally after fifth period there it was, that little envelope icon on my phone that meant there was a message waiting.

I opened it as quickly as I could. "Go ahead", that was my response.

I will! After school? No, I didn't want to wait that long! A quick e mail to the Beagle Freedom Project would make me feel better. Better yet! I will fill out the application and send it. It will only take a second. The website had pictures of some of the Beagles that were available for adoption. I chose the three that I liked the best, although any of them would've been great. Not being an incredibly computer savvy individual, I couldn't, for the life of me, figure out how to send the application. This was going to be more involved than I thought; it would have to wait until I got home.

I tried to send the application again from my fancy laptop at home with no luck. I called my sister, Gwen, for help. I emailed the answers to the application to her so she could fill it out and send it for me. I also asked Bert, during our nightly phone call, if Jay could help me out and gave him the website so he could check out the pictures of our perspective adoptees. In the meantime, I emailed the founder of the organization and explained my dilemma. I also called the number on the website and left a message, explaining my dilemma. All I could do now was wait…I'm not good at that!

I really wanted this to happen NOW because I was about to be on Winter Break for two weeks. You couldn't ask for better timing. However, it wasn't to be. I waited a day or two and started to panic. I checked the website, my e mail, my cell phone, and my home phone constantly. I found every possible e mail listed on the website and emailed it; every possible phone number and called it; every place to make a comment and commented. Nothing was working! My patience was disappearing but I felt like there was nothing I could do. Even if all the Beagles were already placed in forever homes, I just wanted to know something. Anything!

It was the last Friday of school for two weeks; my perfectly timed plan was falling apart! I hadn't heard anything. A friend of mine asked if maybe Bert was secretly working on this as a Christmas present for me, I didn't want to get my hopes up! I'm sure by now, everyone, including Bert, was tired of hearing me talk about the Beagles from Spain and how much I wanted one and how frustrated I was about not hearing anything. I decided to try and relax about it, if it was going to happen it would just happen, right?

Chapter 3

And So It Begins

"One more time," I said to myself. I had found one last place on the website that I hadn't posted a comment to. I pleaded my case in the message portion;

"We want to be a forever home to a Beagle from Spain. I have e mailed, sent an application, and made phone calls and haven't heard anything. Did we miss our chance? Please let me know."

Send.

I didn't really expect anything to happen so when my cell phone rang within one minute of the send button being pressed, I didn't make any connections. I didn't recognize the number so I didn't answer it. Then my home phone rang, I let the machine pick it up, but went to the machine to listen to the message…"Hi Kris, this is Shannon from the Beagle Freedom Project…" Holy Cow! I fumbled with the phone and told her I was on the line.

The next few minutes were unforgettable! First, Shannon apologized for not getting back to me. I guess three people dealing with forty Beagles was a pretty good excuse. She let me know that "Bagel" had just been returned from his foster home and was available for us to meet. Bagel was one of the three I had originally chosen out of the ones that were still available. Of course, not asking where she was located, or checking the time, or thinking beyond anything but saving Bagel, I told her we would be there today.

North Hollywood...certainly not very close.

I convinced Bert to go with me, got directions and kissed our Beagles good bye. The traffic was horrible. Even worse going the other way, the ride home would be no quicker. The entire ride there I kept thinking about how mad Bert would be that this long, long trip was only to "meet" Bagel, not actually bring him home. My plan was to act as surprised as he was that we couldn't actually bring him home yet. I would worry about that later; I couldn't wait to see him.

Chapter 4

Beagle Freedom Project

We reached our destination after three and a half hours in the truck. We walked up to the house and were greeted by two very happy Pit Bulls in the front yard. Shannon and Jean called to us from the back yard and we headed back to a stack of crates, a big yard, and three crazy dogs. I fell in love instantly!

Bagel was a bit shy but jumped up on to Bert's legs and wanted to be pet. He was a tri-color, with a "carmelly " color on his head and ears, the black was primarily on his back but was mixed with brown and white hair, his feet, tummy, and nose were all white. He had very unique markings on his face and legs. His tail was down as was his head and he skulked around the yard even though the other two dogs were playing around him. He was very skinny and had no muscle tone at all. His balance wasn't great and he didn't know how to use his nose. Shannon told us his feet were so big because he had been standing in the metal cage for five years. He still had his do claws and was smelly. He came over to me to say hi and again, jumped up on my legs to be pet. He wouldn't look you in the eye and had the saddest expression on his face. One of the greatest things about Cowboy and Indian are the multitude of expressions they can create because of their eyebrows. I noticed that Bagel's eyebrows didn't work. He had one expression and one expression only...sad with a touch of worry.

While he was skulking around, occasionally coming by to say hi, we talked with Shannon and Jean to get the full story, and what a story it was. Shannon gave us all the details:

"Beagle Freedom Project had accomplished three rescues before we heard about the Spanish beagles. As you can imagine, it is quite difficult to get laboratories to release dogs.

I was on Facebook when I saw a post that a lab in Barcelona was closing, and that 72 beagles were to be killed unless there was a commitment from a group to take them in 24 hours. I saw the post a few days after the lab had said this. I desperately sprang into action and emailed everyone who had posted this. Of course they were all in Spain where it was only about three o'clock in the morning."

Bert and I were hanging on the edge of our seats as we listened to how the events were unfolding, watching Bagel the entire time thinking about him going through all of this. Shannon went on:

"Finally, a man named Andy from Spain called me! I was thrilled! He asked me if I was for real, and was in shock that I would take in 72 lab beagles. I told him yes; of course I'm for real! Andy told me," Okay, let me tell the lab now before they begin killing and I will call you back." I prayed the killing had not begun."

I think I actually gasped when I heard this part of the story! I looked at Bert and could tell he was surprised by it as well. I couldn't believe they would just kill 72 beagles!

Even though I knew how the story ended (happily luckily) I had to hear the rest of it! Shannon continued:

"There were several people working on this rescue in Spain as well as here. Andy and a woman named Eve who was going to temporarily take them all in pending the flight, as well as some other volunteers and vet techs.

There was a veterinarian that had been contacted by the laboratory vet and told that the beagles were going to be killed because the lab was closing. This vet became the liaison between the lab and the rescuers. Suddenly, the lab stopped communicating with the liaison! Our vet kept trying but there was no response. We bit our nails for five days until the lab finally responded and said they had re-homed 22 dogs and would release the rest to us. They claimed they did not kill them. We are guessing they sold them to another lab, but we pray that they really did get homes for them.

So now we had 50 beagles left. There were some people in Spain who wanted to adopt the beagles, and the activists over there found homes for 10 of them...which meant we were getting 40 sent to us. (Originally there were 41 but there was a miscount in Spain)

I had to commit to the cost of all of this. I had no idea how much it would be...I knew it would be a lot though! But, I didn't care. We were rescuing these beagles and finally giving them the life they deserved!

At first, we tried to get a chartered plane, but the cost was too prohibitive, over $250,000. YIKES! So we ended up hiring a company that specialized in relocating animals to different countries. They had never done a relocation on this large scale and were excited to assist. However, their up-front cost would be $35,000. We did not have this kind of money so I used my credit cards to charge it, hoping and praying donations would come in so I could quickly pay off my cards."

I thought Shannon and Jean were impressive for what they had done, but now that I was hearing the entire story...I thought they were the most exceptional, compassionate people I had ever come across. Holy cow! Putting the flight on her credit cards doing all the research to find a company that specialized in animal relocation...I didn't even know that job existed. I was speechless, all I could say, over and over again, was "oh my gosh" and "I can't believe it". I was frustrated that the fates of 22 of the beagles was unknown...all we could do was hope for the best. There was still so much of the story left...

"We then had to arrange the transport of the beagles from the lab to Eve's facility, which was not easy because it meant dealing with the lab and that was proving more and more difficult. It is required by law that the beagles be sent in special vehicles. It didn't help that we were trying to organize all of this over the holidays so no one was ever available! We also had to order 40 travel crates which took forever because of the holidays and because no company that would deliver to Spain had 40 crates available!

As if that wasn't enough, the lab said the beagles had not been vaccinated! This was a major concern, since they needed to be vaccinated for rabies within ten days of arriving in the states. Furthermore, while we waited for the transport vans and crates, the lab refused to vaccinate while we waited. We even offered to pay, but they refused. So, we had to wait until they were released, at which point the people in Spain arranged for veterinarians to examine all of the beagles, vaccinate them, and declare them healthy for travel and entrance into the United States. The beagles would have to spend almost thirty six hours in transport coming to the United States, and would arrive the day before Thanksgiving 2011.

As soon as the beagles were safe at Eve's and were getting all of the paperwork ready for travel, we went into action here. How would we pick up 40 beagles from the airport? Where would we put 40 beagles while we waited for their fosters and adopters? Luckily, we had a great list of fosters who were waiting to foster a lab beagle. We arranged for as many preapproved fosters to arrive the night of the 23rd as we could get to my house. We built pens in my yard as well as tons of crates and beds in the house in my backyard, which would become known as the "Beagle House". Our volunteers got together and built areas throughout the yard and the house for the beagles, made sure there were 40 bowls, 40 collars, 40 tags, 40 beds, wee wee pads, newspaper, blankets, towels, lots of treats and food. We bought heat lamps, heaters and outdoor lighting. A friend of ours used his company's moving van after measuring it out to be sure it would fit 40 crates.

We arrived at LAX, paperwork in hand, awaiting the plane; we were to pick them up at cargo. After waiting for an hour in the freezing cold, we were told the plane had in fact landed and we had to head over to customs to clear them. Cargo gave us additional paperwork to bring with us to customs. We drove over to customs and waited. When we were called, we told the agents we were there to pick up 40 beagles. They asked us for some type of commercial license, we said, "No we are not breeders or anything like that, we rescued these dogs. We are a nonprofit rescue." They could not fathom this and refused to sign off on them! After several minutes of heart pounding and sweating, a supervisor told us that he would sign off on them. PHEW! What a scary moment that was! When we arrived back at cargo, the beagles were already being delivered to the loading dock. Seeing these angels in their crates, shaking and scared broke my heart, but at the same time, I knew it would be a short time until they were free in America. We loaded all 40 beagles up and we were off!

Once we arrived at my house, it was an assembly line of people lining up the crates. Before we let them out, we had to make sure the number on their collar corresponded with the number on their crate. Through all the travel, we assumed some would probably be put back in the wrong crates. We were concerned about who was who, since there was a lot of confusion in Spain. It did not really matter, but we wanted to be as thorough as we could be.

After cross-checking, we brought them all into my backyard. On the count of three, we released them. Many immediately ran out of their crates, while others stood shaking in their crates and would not exit. Others ran out and hid in the bushes or behind things."

I felt a little silly but at this point in Shannon's retelling I was in tears. All I could picture was these adorable, scared, shaking beagles waiting to come out of their crates, but having no idea what was in store for them. I had to wonder if they thought maybe they were at another lab, Bagel had already been to two labs as proven by the two different tattoos in his ears. I could only imagine how scared and untrusting these poor guys must have been that first night. I felt exhausted just listening to all of this. My heart stopped when the customs agents wouldn't sign off on the beagles, I could just picture all the crates piled up with little faces inside just waiting. I wished I could have been at Shannon's house to help the night they came in, what an experience. Bert and I tried to decide what Bagel might have done when he was released, we decided he was one that ran right out but went right into the bushes. I wanted to hear more.

"It was a mad house! 40 male, un-neutered beagles running around humping, hiding, eating, pooing, peeing, fighting, you name it! It was crazy but we loved every second of it! Luckily, many of the fosters came the first night, so by the time everyone left (about three in the morning), I was left with 18 beagles at my house and our other volunteers took 8 of them.

The next few weeks were intense! Getting good fosters for them (some of them were VERY afraid of people) was difficult, taking care of that many beagles at my house, as well as trying to keep up with the huge amount of emails and calls was overwhelming. Little did we know what we were getting into when this all started! Soon, we would get all 40 adopted into their forever homes and the rest is history..." Shannon wrapped up her incredible recounting with a huge smile on her face.

Well it was still history in the making for us. I completely understood what Shannon was talking about. I knew firsthand how hectic things must have been. After all, I had been one of those phone calls and emails (I guess not just one) that she had to try and keep up with. I was just so glad my persistence had paid off. Looking at Bagel sitting there and realizing everything he had gone through to get here, and what Shannon and her volunteers had gone through to get him here sealed the deal for Bert and me. Phenomenal dogs brought here by phenomenal people, I wanted to be a part of all of this so much. Bagel just had to come home with us.

We found out that Bagel had already been in two foster homes since his "liberation" four weeks ago. The first home he had actually run away from and been on his own for almost 24 hours. He was then sent to another foster home that was in an apartment with a family that worked all day. I didn't ask why he had been returned or why his foster home had "fallen through"; I just knew I wanted to take him home. Still worried that Bert would be upset about leaving empty handed, I talked about how bad the traffic was and how long of a drive it been, hoping that might change policy.

Shannon and Jean were telling us more about Bagel as we watched him. She said he was a "bolter" and that was how he had escaped from his first foster family; she told us we needed to be careful when we opened doors. We tried to ease their minds by telling them we lived on five fenced acres and there was no way he would be able to get out. She let us know that he was not potty trained yet because they had just gone in their crates for the last five years, and asked if that would be a problem for us. "Not at all"' we both answered, we have a doggie door and the other three dogs would help him figure it out. I talked about the nature of Bert's work and how Bagel would be able to run and hunt like a Beagle should. We talked about Cowboy, Indian and Jager and the dog dynamics at our house. I explained that our dogs were our children, our very spoiled, well taken care of children. I told them that I take the horses out for trail rides and all the dogs come along for some fun.

Wow! I wanted to be one of our dogs.

I was hoping I had them convinced. I asked what the process was to adopt Bagel. Shannon made sure to correct me, "We foster to adopt," she said, "are you interested in that?"

I looked at Bert, he looked at me…"Definitely", we said together.

Shannon told us that usually this would just be a meet and greet and they would bring Bagel when they did the "home visit", but because we had come so far, they would send him home with us today. Whew! I was off the hook, no explaining to do. We talked about his care and feeding, got a little care package full of toys and treats, hooked him to a leash and we were off.

Chapter 5

Going Home

He walked really well on a leash. Better than any of our dogs, that was for sure. We walked across the street to my very large Ford F-250. If we hadn't convinced them yet of our love of Beagles, my license plate sealed the deal…BEGLLMO (Beagle Limo). We decided we needed to have a picture of Bagel in the bed of the truck with his paws over the tailgate above the license plate. He was going to have to get used to his photo being taken… I think he actually posed.

We said our goodbyes and headed out. The first thing Bert and I did, once we were alone with the "new guy", was talk about his name. I call the Beagles bagels occasionally but this guy needed a great name of his own. We had a Cowboy, an Indian …Tonto, Marshall, Scout, Chief, Ranger…so many choices. We laughed a lot about the nick names that would be derived from any of these names. After all, Indian had turned into Shmin, occasionally Shmini Marie (don't ask), Cowboy had turned into Cowboy Jones then into Dr. Jones (again, don't ask). We finally decided on Chieftan, Chief for short.

It took him a while to settle down in the truck. The stop and go traffic kept throwing him into the dashboard because his balance was so bad. His huge spread out paws kept slipping on the leather seats and leaving little sweaty paw marks everywhere. A new nick name was already coming to me. After about a half hour, he curled up between Bert and me and fell asleep. I took tons of pictures with my phone to send to EVERYONE we know. I finally got just the right one of him and sent it with the message "New rescue from Spain on the way home!" I was flooded with responses about our new addition. Chief really didn't like the ringtone I had for text messages, a bunch of tweeting birds; he kept waking up every time I would get one. He finally cuddled up close enough so he could lay his head on my lap. I melted; I actually think Bert may have too.

The trip home was long and slow. The whole way home Bert and I talked about the horrible things poor Chief must have gone through. Shannon told us she knew that he was used for human drug testing but that was all she knew. I noticed he actually had dents in the pads on his feet from standing on the metal grate of the floor of his cage. We were in total disbelief that he had been in a cage from the time he was taken from his mom to now. The things he had never seen, smelled, heard, and tasted. It was impossible not to be really sad and upset. But at the same time incredibly happy and proud that we were on the way home with this special dog to finally let him experience all of these things.

Chapter 6

Release the hounds

My husband and I are fortunate enough to have my mother, Gale, living on our property in a house about fifty feet from ours. She is a wonderful woman, and has slowly gone from city dweller to country dweller and from cats only to cats, dogs, and horses. She is a great help around the "ranch" and allows us the freedom to do many things we wouldn't otherwise be able to do if she wasn't there to hold down the fort.

Before we reached home, I called my mom to let her know we were almost there. The plan was to lock all the dogs up in the house so Chief would be able to get out of the truck and be on his own for a moment before he was accosted by two crazy Beagles and an old, grouchy bird dog. Unfortunately, by the time we got home it was dark and very cold. Bert got out and headed down to feed the horses, Chief got out and followed right behind him. Not really knowing what a horse was…Chief walked right up to our very kind, mellow Thoroughbred, Homes, sniffed noses and walked away like it was nothing! We would soon find out that was not a good thing. We discovered that he trots everywhere, even when he's not sure where he's going. So he trotted back up to the house behind Bert.

We released the hounds! They are always so excited to see us, like we've been gone forever, and in their frenzy to say hello, they didn't even notice the new guy. Amazingly and happily enough the whole butt sniffing introduction ritual went off with not much of a hitch. Our dogs are all very good with other dogs but sometimes they get a bit territorial when they are at home. Not this time. Chief was not at all fazed by having three dogs come at him at once. So far so good.

The next test was about to begin...the house. I love dogs, everything about them, but I never want my house to smell like I have dogs. So peeing in the house is a huge no no in my book. Cowboy, the most perfect dog in the world, was the easiest to potty train. Indian on the other hand, was a nightmare. Almost to the point of experiencing buyer's remorse. But we got over that and I have not really had to think about "that" in five years. Things were about to change.

The whole world changed the moment we entered the house. Cows suddenly turned into a territorial "land shark", barking if Chief came near one single toy or our bedroom door. Trying to protect every toy as well as cover the door made for some serious action throughout the house. Indian was very agreeable and welcoming and good, old Jager could not have cared less. I was worried most about how Cowboy would take our new family member. He is one of the most sensitive dogs I have ever met and the last thing I wanted to do was make any of the dogs, especially Cowboy, feel second to the new guy.

Bert thinks I'm a bit on the crazy side because I am positive that all of my animals have feelings like people do and react to things the way I would. We all have conversations, which I'm sure they understand. So when I took Cowboy aside to explain Chief's sad history and that our job was to welcome him into our home and make his life as great as his was, I truly believe he understood. I thanked Indian for being such a great host and told him he had a new playmate, although he was going to have to teach him how to play. I don't talk to Jager very much, not only because he probably can't hear me (he's nineteen years old), but I'm pretty sure he wouldn't really care about what I had to say.

Another test...dinner time. Each dog has his own "spot" for dinner. Cowboy and Indian eat together in the living room and Jager eats in the kitchen. Chief's spot would be in the kitchen with Jager. I wasn't really sure how much he had been getting, not enough in my opinion (I like my animals "healthy") so I gave him what they all got. Holy cow! I don't know that I had ever seen anything like watching Chief eat. He didn't know how. He would press his nose down into the bowl and mash all of the food together. He was using his front teeth to chew so anything extra would fall out of the sides of his mouth. He was hungry though, and didn't give up. He ate and ate and ate...he cleaned all of the bowls there was not a speck of food to be found.

I was trying to get dinner started for us when all of a sudden Bert said "He's peeing!" Right on the new leather chair I had given Bert for our anniversary. I took a deep breath, I didn't want to scare Chief but I wanted to let him know that it was not okay to pee in the house. We just moved on past this one and I quickly cleaned it up. I managed to get dinner in the oven while Bert followed him around from room to room keeping a close eye on him. Or so I thought...

When Bert came out of the bedroom with his shirt pulled up over his nose and mouth I knew something bad had just happened. Bert is an incredibly tough man, but when it comes to yucky smelly things, he is no help at all! I had just checked the oven so I wouldn't burn dinner and then got the story. "He just exploded in the bedroom!" Bert moaned to me through his shirt, "One second he was just sniffing around, the next BOOM! It's everywhere!" And it was! I went to work cleaning up one of the smelliest, biggest piles I had honestly ever seen. Bert took him outside but, it was obviously a bit late for that! We thought, between the long car ride, the stress of meeting 3 new dogs, new food and a lot of it, a new house, and any number of other things, poor Chief was bound to explode. We were going to have to be very patient, observant, and diligent with our potty training.

We were both able to grab some dinner on the fly, between following Chief around and taking him outside if he looked like he might need to do anything. We, humans and canines alike, were all exhausted and definitely ready for bed.

Chapter 7

Yet another test

Bed...yet another test! Bert wanted to barricade him in the bathroom, I of course vehemently disagreed, he'd been cooped up enough in his lifetime, and it wouldn't happen again if I could help it! He would sleep on the bed with the rest of us! A wise, veteran Beagle owner once told us that once the Beagle starts sleeping in the bed...your love life would be over. Well, now we had three! Jager slept on the floor in a very cushy sheepskin bed, he could no longer get up the steps to reach our ridiculously high bed. Cowboy and Indian each had their respective spots on the bed. Cowboy, when not under the covers, was curled up near one of our stomachs, Indian, was a pillow sleeper, and stayed up at the head of the bed for most of the night. Chief would have to carve out a niche for himself.

Although I wanted Chief on the bed for purely altruistic reasons, it was also to make it easier for me to see when he needed to get up throughout the night. Bert sleeps like a rock and I was quite sure it was going to be me and me only on night patrol. I was actually surprised how many times he got up. He is a quick pee-er and he tricked me a few times. We would go outside, walk around, sometimes he would go sometimes he wouldn't. Then we would get back into bed for another couple hours, before our next outing. As I had suspected, Bert, or the dogs for that matter, never stirred! I probably got about 4 hours of sleep total that night and we had only had three accidents.

Day 2

Chapter 8

Progress

I took Chief out with me in the morning to feed the horses. His tail was still down but his little face looked "softer" than it had the day before. He readily followed me everywhere, but as soon as I started to move the wheel barrow full of hay, he bolted. It is a very loud, clanking, metallic sounding wheel barrow, so it was completely understandable that he would be afraid. He followed me at a distance down to the horses and sniffed noses with our young, overzealous, Thoroughbred, Norman and Homes again. Both of these horses were brought up playing with Indian, so they are both really good with dogs, my concern was, that all the horses we had were not so good with dogs. He kept a wide berth from the wheel barrow on the way back to the house but followed me right in…after stopping to pee one more time before we went in. Progress.

As I was making coffee, everyone else started to make their way out of the bedroom. Bert asked how it had gone, and as I was explaining how many times we had gotten up and that he was actually pretty good… he lifted his leg on one of the Christmas presents under the tree! We both said together, "uh uh!" in fairly loud voices. He stopped right away and didn't look too scared. More progress.

He was hungry again. So I poured out some dry food for him. Gone. "He eats like a horse!" Bert said, "There goes our dog food bill, we'll keep our local feed store in business, that's for sure!" I was hoping the other dogs would start to figure out that there would be no more leisurely dining. With Chief around they had to go right to their bowls and eat, whether they were ready or not. Cowboy liked to wait and see what we were having for dinner, before he decided to accept dog food as his meal. I've actually only been able to find two things that Cowboy will not eat, water chestnuts and bananas. Indian was a very persnickety eater, and only did so when he was in the mood. Jager was the only one that actually ate when he was fed.

Bert and I both noticed the slight change in his facial expression but also how much more confident he seemed about his new house. He would trot from room to room sniffing and exploring; with one of us following at all times of course. At one point he came out of Bert's bathroom carrying a glove. Was he playing? He carried it around for a moment and then lost interest when he spied my favorite sheepskin slippers. Off limits. All of a sudden he grabbed one and took off across the bedroom, his tail wasn't all the way up but it was higher than it had been. I didn't want to break his concentration so I whispered to Bert to come watch him "play". I decided to break out one of the dog's Christmas presents (a furry leopard spotted snake) to give Chief something other than my slipper to play with. "Awww, puppy's first toy!" I told Bert. He just gave me that, "you're coo coo" look, he does so well. Chief was having a blast. So much progress. We had an accident or two in the house that morning, but he would always stop "mid-stream" when he was caught and gently reprimanded.

Chapter 9

New Trials

Time to get outside to start on chores. All of the dogs jump through the dog door as soon as anyone goes towards the laundry room. Chief obviously didn't understand where they had all gone. He stood in front of the dog door and just stared at it. If no one comes out after a certain amount time, all the dogs will pile back through the door to see what's going on. So with poor Chief standing right in front of the door, two Beagles and a bird dog came blasting through and knocked him right over. If he wasn't afraid of the door before, he was now. Bert went outside and held the dog door open, I stayed inside and tried to get Chief to go through it...he was not having any of it. We decided he was going to experience many new things that day, and we had plenty of time to work on the dog door. It was time to move on.

We went out to move horses from one pen to a bigger pasture and all the dogs went off to do what dogs do. Chief was on his own and "patrolled" the entire fence line of the property. He trotted the entire way around stopping occasionally to sniff something or look out past the fence. I have never been preoccupied with my dog's bathroom habits, but I was really happy to see him lift a leg a few times. He would come by and visit but spent most of his time exploring. He even ventured out into the pasture with all five

Oh so serious

Chief's face had no expression

horses at one point. Being quite clueless about horses, there was Chief, standing in the middle of four horses all sniffing him at the same time. He didn't move. I wasn't sure what had captivated his attention to the point of not noticing he was surrounded. I would discover later it was the delicacy of horse manure that he had discovered. When he finally did look up, he bolted. That was a good sign. I liked that he was somewhat afraid.

Chief followed me in the house and to my surprise had already figured out where to stand to beg for a cookie. Because of his strange eating habits, Chief leaves most of his cookie on the floor. Cowboy is our cookie "Hoover" and is more than happy to clean up after everyone. Indian likes to take his treats to another spot, sometimes it's the bedroom, sometimes the couch, sometimes a rug but wherever he ends up, he waits patiently with his treat on the floor in front of him for someone to break it into small, bite sized pieces. Jager just grabs them from your hand and inhales them.

Bert decided to take everyone out for a short ride in the truck. We realized that every time poor Chief had been for a ride he had left a home and not returned. Our dogs spend a lot of time travelling whether is to Bert's job sites or to Montana or Michigan for the summer. They have all had to figure out that sleeping is the best way to travel. Bert wanted Chief to understand that we were his people and this was his home. So from now on when he left…this is where he would come back to. All of the dogs piled into Bert's truck, Jager has to be lifted in but Cows and Indian usually jump right in. Chief had to be lifted, but just piled in with everyone else. His social skills were lacking in many areas, one of which was going around something in his way or sitting in a spot that was vacant. Instead, he would boar right in, over and on anything or anyone that was in his way. Indian likes to sit in the driver's seat, Cows vacillates between shotgun and the back seat with Jager, and Jager usually takes up the entire back seat. So, just like the bed, Chief was going to have to find a spot to call his own. It was a short trip to a ranch down the road and Chief took the front seat with Cowboy and Indian. He was calm and quiet even when the ranch dogs ran out to greet the truck. They were only there a few moments then returned home. Everyone piled out of the truck and I was so happy to have Chief trot up to me with his tail up and wagging. Amazing progress.

Chapter 10

New Nicknames

It had been a long first day for Chief, physically and mentally, I was sure. By the end of the day, we noticed that he was very lame on his front feet. His poor pads were very tender and, after five years in a cage, not used to all the running around on dirt, pebbles and the occasional sticker. Except for a quick snooze here and there, he hadn't slept or slowed down all day. He was getting better with the doggie door but wasn't really interested in going inside unless one of us was in there. Indian was starting to get him to play "chase", and we were seeing his tail up and wagging more and more. Bert and I noticed that Chief's eyebrows were becoming operational. We had seen a few more expressions and he was starting to look less anxious and happier. But still hungry.

Dinnertime. Second round, Chief already understood the drill. I noticed the sweaty paw prints on the slate floor while he was waiting for his bowl. The new nickname came to me...Chief Sweaty Feet. He was obviously starving, even after a breakfast and lunch time snack. He ate in his "spot" alternating between standing and sitting, but took a tour of all the other bowls soon after licking the design off of his own. Cowboy and Indian still hadn't gotten the memo that they needed to eat when they were served or else "piggywoggins" (which Bert had fondly nick named Cowboy before the new guy came home) would help himself to their bowls.

After dinner, Chief hopped up onto the couch to stake his claim at the end with the pillow. He had formally become a member of the "Beagle Train". Indian on one end, Cows in the middle and Chief on the other end. The small spot I was allowed to inhabit was now gone. Good thing I didn't mind sitting on the floor. As he lay there, Bert and I noticed how huge his stomach was. He looked like he was about to burst. We didn't think it was possible, but he looked like he had actually already gained weight, quite a bit of it. After a short time Chief got up, jumped down from the couch and practically threw himself on to the hard wood floor. Of course I interpreted this as him not being used to being on something soft and comfy and needing to be uncomfortable. Bert told me it was probably just because he was hot and wanted a cool surface to lie on. That made sense too.

We actually got to sit down to dinner that night, but had forgotten to take him out and had an accident. We blamed ourselves and made sure he went out a few more times before bed. He didn't always want to go out and would always grab a bite for the road, when there was anything left to grab. I had to carry him out one last time but when he peed I was glad I had. Two Beagles and one adult already in bed, it would be a tight squeeze but I was more than happy to do it. Chief had completely stolen my heart, Bert and my mom's too. I was so happy that we had made this decision even as I was contorting my body into the most uncomfortable position so I wouldn't disturb any of the Beagles. Note to self: Be the first one in bed.

It was only about an hour before Chief was up and I was right behind him. He helped himself to some water while I

Beagle Train

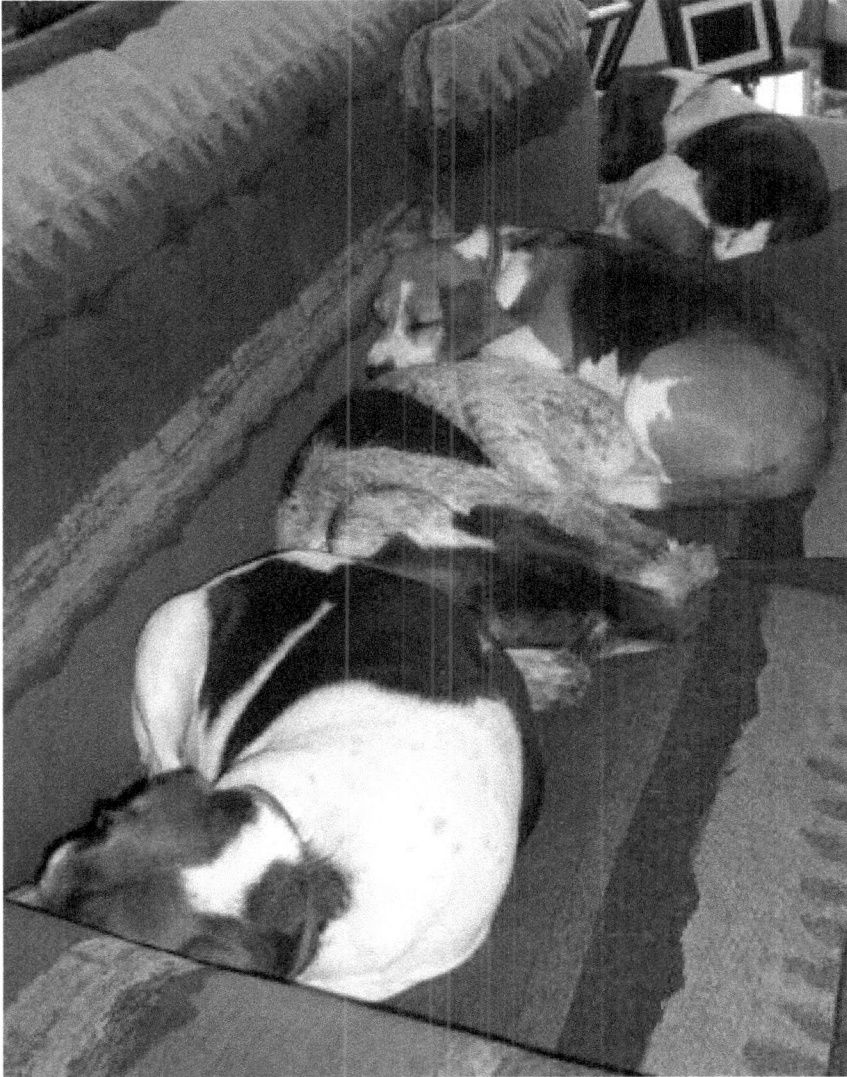

Chief managed to squeeze himself into the Beagle train.

piled all my jackets, hats and gloves on to take him outside. Once back inside, he went for the couch. I curled up next to him on the couch for another few hours before Indian and Jager came flying out of the bedroom barking and sliding on the wood floor to get to the doggie door as fast as possible. Unfortunately, this is a nighttime ritual when the coyotes are active outside. Cowboy doesn't usually participate unless it's a serious sounding bark, preferring his beauty sleep to chasing coyotes, but Indian and usually Jager will fly at any noise. Back on the couch, poor Chief had a nervous breakdown and didn't know if he should follow, stay, or what. Right away, his anxious face came back. I sat and cuddled with him for a moment when Indian came back in and joined us on the couch. Everything seemed to settle down and we all curled up for a few more hours sleep.

Luckily the couch is fairly comfortable so sleeping most of the night on it wasn't too bad. The bad part was getting up two or three more times to take Chief out into the frigid night air to go potty or just walk around. After the last time, we went into the bedroom and curled up in bed with Bert, Cowboy and Indian, and just like the night before, Bert and Cowboy hadn't moved for the majority of the night. We got a few good hours of sleep in bed before it was time to get up and feed horses. Bert took morning duty and brought all the hounds out with him while he fed.

Chapter 11

ARRROOOO!

I have no idea how it could have possibly happened, or how Bert could have walked right passed the small lake of pee on the kitchen floor. I thought I had been with him during every waking moment last night…another nick name Chief Sneaky Peer. I was about to be upset with Chief when he went sprinting past me with his tail up and my slipper in his mouth. I quickly followed him back into the bedroom where he had spun around to face me with his butt up in the air, tail wagging furicusly, slipper between his front two paws, and a smile (yes, a smile) on his face. I was laughing so hard I scared him, but he didn't try to run, he just stepped away from the slipper.

Bert really noticed a difference in his face today. Chief loves to put his front paws up onto our thighs and stretch up for a scratch. Bert said, as he was scratching under his collar," I can't believe the difference in his face! It's softer… happier, he just looks so different! I can't wait for the Beagle People to see him." His eyebrows were fully functional by this time and he was even starting to do the adorable "who me?" head cock, when he heard anything unfamiliar. The anxious, worried face came back occasionally, especially when the other hounds would bolt out of the house baying at the top of their lungs. He became very worried if anyone put on a jacket while standing over him or when the overhead fans were turned on when he was directly under them. I found it interesting to note the things that scared him, the noises or quick movements, some things made more sense than others and it always brought me back to the horrible things he had been through.

Chief's talents with the doggie door were improving every day and he no longer needed coaxing to go in or come out. We still hadn't heard him bark, and Shannon had told us that some of the rescues may have been debarked but the only way to tell was to wait and see. So, that morning when he went flying out the doggie door to Bert's truck parked in a different spot, much closer than before, and Bert and my mom standing there chatting, to our surprise he let out the biggest, loudest, Beagle howl we had heard from him. It was the greatest sound. Bert ran in the house to ask if I had heard it, I had of course, you could have heard it for miles, but when he told me it was Chief, I was ecstatic! Well, the flood gates were open…he was no longer shy about his God given gift to howl. He was now keeping up with the other two.

We decided to take him for a walk in the field across the road from our house. I always take the horses out for trail rides across the road and the dogs come with me for some running and hunting. We wanted to see what Chief would do out in the wide open spaces on his own (with Bert close by). The area is covered with tall sage brush, redshank, and other various shrubs so losing sight of him would be very easy. I took my mare, Mama, out first with all the other dogs bounding out of the gate in front of me. Bert had Chief on a leash and walked him out the gate. He was not very interested in staying with the other dogs, which was unfortunate, although it had only been a few days and he may not have figured out that this was his new family. I rode on and the dogs disappeared into the bushes after one scent or another.

Moments like this made me reflect on how we had trained the other two Beagles to stay with me while I was riding. They rarely stayed right with me, but always went in the general direction I was going, and always came back to the house not long after I returned. We had gotten Cowboy and Indian as puppies, and Bert had Jager long before we were together. I think Jager did most of the training, Cowboy and Indian both had been tied to him at some stage so they would learn to come when they were called and not roam too far. I would like to take some of the credit for our well behaved Beagles but Bert was always the one to take them to work and deal with the "being free" aspect of our lifestyle. It always stressed me out too much to just let them go and hope for the best. But, however it was done our training methods worked great on puppies that were neutered at a young age…hopefully they would work on a five year old "puppy" that had only been neutered for three weeks.

Bert eventually let Chief off the leash to see what he would do. He set off in a very purposeful trot in no particular direction, not really using his nose for anything. Bert didn't mind the possibility of losing sight of him out there…it would prove to be too stressful for me. He worked on trying to get Chief to follow him, "trying" being the key word here. But, we decided for his first try in the wilds, he did a great job.

When we were all back on the property and locked in the fun began.

Bert is one of those individuals that is good at just about everything he does. He is an amazing builder and was responsible for building my mom's house; all the shelters for our horses, as well as an amazing deck that, when finished, will stretch across the entire front of our house. While he was on a short "vacation" from the horse show season, he was finishing up the roof on another section of the deck. All I can say is, Chief was "helping". He took boxes of nails, gloves, Bert's tool belt, scraps of wood, dragged tools around by the cords, and I'm sure many other things we didn't even see happen. New nick name...Chief the thief. I think Bert spent more time collecting his tools than he did working on the roof.

Chief and Indian had really started to get along and Indian had actually gotten him to start joining him in his famous "psycho circles". These were the circles that Indian did at a million miles an hour all over the property, between trees, in and out of the pastures, sometimes with toys in his mouth, or sticks (that always worries me). Chief had just started to chase him for a short way before giving up and not really understanding the purpose. Indian would keep trying to get him going, sometimes it would work sometimes it wouldn't. For the remainder of the afternoon, after lunch of course, Chief and the other dogs crashed on the lawn while Bert worked on the deck and I ran around doing chores.

We all headed inside for the evening...what a great day! So much progress, between the howling, the playing, the "trail ride", NO ACCIDENTS, the doggie door, the happy face, and so many more accomplishments we didn't even see, Chief's learning curve was on an accelerated up swing. I noticed while I was getting dinner ready for the dogs...Chief was about asleep on his feet. His eyes were just about closed, he was weaving back and forth, and his head was actually bobbing up and down. New nick name...Chief Sleepy Face. However, as soon as I put his bowl down...he was fully conscious and ready to eat. He hit all the bowls buffet style but luckily the other dogs were starting to figure out his M.O. and they were eating when they were fed.

The Beagle train had formed on the couch and all was quiet, for the moment. I was in the kitchen getting dinner ready when Bert called me into the family room. "He's dreaming, he's dreaming, come look at him! "He whispered. Chief was stretched out in his spot, his paws were twitching, his nose and eyes were twitching, and he was making a very faint whining sound. I hoped he was dreaming about his great day and not having flashbacks of his recent past. I had heard two theories on the memory of dogs: they have no long term memory and live in the moment and they had memories more like ours and could remember the past. For Chief's sake I was hoping the first was true.

If you haven't figured it out yet...our dogs are ridiculously spoiled and are the children we never had, they are my mother's "grand dogs", and my sister is the auntie that spoils them when she comes to town. So when we sit down for dinner, although exceptionally polite while they do it, they beg for goodies. It made perfect sense for Chief to follow suit. Without any lessons, Chief had become the perfectly polite table beggar. New nick name Chief ya gunna eat that? While we ate dinner he waited patiently by the table, Cows and Indian on the couch waiting patiently as well, and Jager usually asleep until the food was actually being distributed (which I still find amazing that he knows when to wake up as he can't see, hear, or smell very well anymore). We discovered Chief's not much into plain carbs, like bread or potatoes, (he really didn't care for crumpets) very much like Indian. Cowboy and Jager on the other hand eat just about everything. Chief had a very difficult time chewing things that were too big or too hard and made a mess on the floor which Cowboy was more than happy to clean up for him. Cowboy and Indian are the designated "plate lickers" it worked out perfectly, two plates...two lickers. Now we had one more tongue. Bert put his plate down for Chief, much to Cowboy's dismay, but he did not understand the whole licking thing. Cowboy politely pushed him over and showed him how it was done.

Dinner dishes were put up and all the food was gone, so the dogs were all crashed in their respective spots. Chief's sleeping routine included getting down off the couch after awhile and throwing himself on the wood floor by Bert's chair. In awhile, he would get up again and find his spot on the couch or in Jager's chair. He had been so great with the potty training; we hadn't had any accidents since the beginning. After dinner, in the evening, he usually made us aware that he needed one more trip out before bed by releasing the most horrid stench we had ever smelled! Cowboy and Indian had already taught us that Beagles are gassy little critters, but this was mind blowing. The first few times we experienced the pungent odor, Bert and I actually walked around the house looking for the evidence. We finally realized it was Chief's friendly reminder that he needed to go out one more time.

We all piled into bed, everyone in their spots and settled in for our first FULL night of sleep. Tomorrow would bring new adventures with the first visit from my sister and her husband for the beginning of the Christmas celebrations.

Chapter 12

Complete Craziness

It was Christmas Eve and I had all sorts of baking to do so we got an early start. Chief followed me outside to feed the horses and I noticed how close he followed me everywhere I went. Occasionally he would bump me with his nose to let me know he was still there. The potty training was complete but I really wished I could have used the nick name of Chief Sneaky Pooher. All the other dogs were wonderfully discreet about where they poohed, using the acreage far away from the house. Chief, on the other hand, went anywhere and everywhere. In the five years we had been on this property I rarely ever had to pick up poops, not anymore. It had become almost a daily chore since Chief came home. But if that was the worst thing...I didn't mind. At least he was doing it outside.

Indian came outside with us while Cows opted to stay in bed. Indian and Chief took off to "patrol" the fence line and I headed inside. I loved that he was becoming a bit more independent and was ok with being outside on his own. He and Indian burst in through the doggie door and I noticed he had something in his mouth as he ran by to the bedroom. Bert's shoe. When I followed him into the bedroom he no longer was interested in the shoe and took off. He zigged, then zagged and went for my bathroom. Two seconds later he came running out, tail up and wagging with my jeans in tow, through the door towards the kitchen. When the jeans caught on a chair and practically jerked him off his feet he dropped them and kept going. This went on for about five minutes. He was completely crazy! I was laughing hysterically at this Beagle dragging article after article of clothing out from my and Bert's bathrooms. Note to self...don't leave things on the floor.

Chief sat in the kitchen and watched my every move while I was baking pies for Christmas Eve dinner. But when Bert headed out to move horses around he was the first one to move. I was starting to notice something very interesting in Chief's behavior, and of course ascribed my own interpretation to it. Whenever someone was heading outside and all the dogs made the move to go, Chief would always check the food bowls and eat anything that was left before he would go. I was sure it was because he was afraid there would be no more food coming so he had to fill up while he could. Remnants of his sad past life in the lab, where he obviously did not get enough to eat. After being called a few times from the door he would eventually leave the bowl and join the pack.

Chapter 13

Horsing Around

Outside, Bert was leading our young horse, Norman down to another pen for the day. Norman was raised playing with Indian and I have even caught him playing with Indian's favorite toy which is a gray, squeaky squirrel. The two of them actually played together with the squirrel trying to keep it away from each other, I stood mesmerized watching the two of them one morning, and it was like something out of a Disney movie. Needless to say, Norman is very good around the dogs, but the dogs are very respectful of his size. Chief hadn't quite learned that respect yet. While Bert was walking Norman, Chief fell right into step directly in front of him. Norman put his head down to sniff the new member of the family, and being a gangly youngster, started to lose his balance and speed up. Chief, being a clueless about horse youngster, wasn't paying attention to the large animal quickly approaching him from behind. In the blink of an eye, Chief was rolling across the ground squealing, and Norman was doing everything he could not to step on him. Bert quickly checked Chief out and determined that all the noise was just out of fear not pain. Hopefully, he had learned his lesson...

We also discovered today that aggressive dogs do not seem to bother Chief at all; in fact, he can't be bothered by them. Our neighbors have three big dogs that occasionally walk our fence line and try to get our dogs going. Indian seems to think he is an awful lot bigger and tougher than he really is and will always participate in if not instigate the fence fighting with the neighbor dogs. Of course the sound draws Cowboy, who usually hangs back, and Jager, who is also an instigator, to the fence. Chief followed because that's what he does now. His face was pressed up against the fence, right in the middle of the "fight" and he just stood still for a moment, silently, and then trotted off. New nick name, Chief Whatever!

Today seemed to be a day of discovery! For only being around for a few days, Chief had already figured out where the cookie jar inside was, and now where the apple cookies for the horses were. Our horse trailer is parked near the house and I use it to store my equipment and supplies, as well as a place to get the horses ready; until Bert builds a barn for me (in his spare time). In the dressing room I keep the stash of apple flavored horse cookies that the dogs have become quite fond of. Going in and out of the trailer for various reasons, Chief now understood why Cowboy would wait at the door...treats. He would now be standing by the door when anyone was close by or even when they were not so close by, just hoping for a treat. I of course would go out of my way to go in the trailer to get one for him.

Chapter 14

Visitors

A new test was going to be given this afternoon…visitors. My sister and her husband, Rick, were coming up for a few days to spend the holidays in the "country". Chief had only experienced Bert, my mom, and I so far, so the addition of two more people in the house would be interesting. They got to the house around 4:00 so things around the house were starting to wind down, the horses were tucked in for the evening and the dogs were being fed. My sister, Rick, and my mom all came in together…Cowboy, Indian, and Jager usually bark at visitors and run to the door that they come in, so as usual, they did. Whoa! That was all too much for the new guy. He didn't know what to do, where to go, if he should bark or not, his worried face was back in an instant and he just froze. As soon as I pointed out to my visitors that we had just scared Chief to death, everyone quieted down, my sister and I knelt down and called him over to us quietly. He came over to us with his tail down and worried face on, but as soon as my sister started to pet him and talk to him, he turned back into his new self. Chief wasn't quite sure about the new guests and was more worried about Rick than my sister. Shannon had told us that often times the rescue dogs were more afraid of men than women. I hadn't noticed it with Bert but I was really seeing it with Rick. Luckily Rick was patient and a big fan of Indian's so it didn't take long for Chief to warm up to him.

We were going to be having Christmas Eve dinner over at my mom's house, which meant the dogs would sit outside her house and bark. This would be the first time Chief was going to be "almost" left alone. It was very cold outside and I decided to put Jager's blanket on because I didn't want him to freeze. At one point I had bought matching blue blankets for Cowboy and Jager, they were tough, miniature versions of horse blankets. Unfortunately, Cowboy grew a bit bigger than we had anticipated and his no longer fit, he didn't really like to wear it anyway. I thought I would try it on Chief because I knew he would probably sit outside with the others and wouldn't be used to the near freezing temperatures of December.

Not even thinking, I walked up to Chief holding the blanket like a tunnel for him to just put his head through like I always had for Cowboy and Jager. Note to self…THINK! Again I scared him to death and he backed up as fast as he could with worried face back on. The light bulb in my brain came on and I realized what I had just done. I unfastened the clip that went around the neck so the blanket was completely flat. I let him take a look at it and slowly put it on his back, he tried to dart forward, but I was holding on to his collar. We took a moment, I was whispering to him, he was looking at me like I was crazy and I finally got the front strap fastened. From there it was easy to get the two belly straps fastened. When he was all strapped in, he took off acting incredibly frisky. I thought it was just Jager that did that, he always takes off bucking and rearing when he gets his blanket on, it was great to see Chief doing the same thing. We were off to dinner.

Just like I thought, Chief stayed outside with all the other dogs, he may not have contributed to the serenade but he was there. Bert went out to feed hay to the horses and the whole pack followed him out and ran around him like they hadn't seen him in weeks. Chief was in the middle of it with his tail up and wagging.

Another great day for Chief. It was time for bed so we took him out one last time and all jumped into bed to dream of sugar plums. His spot seemed to be at the end of the bed, more in the corner, on Bert's side, which worked out perfectly with the other dogs. Bert on the other hand was a little cramped, but willing to make the sacrifice. We weren't asleep for long when we both woke up to a loud thud. Bert said, "I think the new guy just fell off the bed!" I didn't think it was him, I thought he was stretched out next to me, "No," I said, "I think that was Shmin." Bert, being an intelligent individual, just turned the light on to find our answer. Sure enough, there was Indian, stretched out next to me and there was poor, in shock, Chief sitting on the floor just staring into space. I felt so bad for him, here he finally came up onto the bed all on his own, he picked his own spot, he was going to sleep through the night (hopefully), and boom!, off he went onto the floor. Of course, I had to ask Bert if he had kicked him or pushed him off, I knew better...just had to check. I made Bert pick him up and put him back in bed, a bit further from the edge this time, and we all tried again. A perfect night, we didn't get up once after that!

Chapter 15

Merry Christmas

Christmas Day! My and my family's favorite holiday of the year. Chief had made it through another night. We would have to delete the nick name Chief Sneaky Peer from his list and replace it with Chief Big Bladder. He was up with all of us ready to go out and do morning chores, after a quick snack of course. When we came back in and the whole family was over, he became a bit overwhelmed again. He wasn't fond of the loud bursts of laughter, that we are guilty of when we get together, or all the people moving around. But to my complete surprise, his worried, anxious face didn't really reappear. His tail wasn't up all the way and he skulked around the house more than walked but he was able to mingle with my sister and her husband really well. Bert was in the kitchen making his famous chicken fried steak and eggs for breakfast and Chief just sat in the kitchen waiting and watching. When we sat down to eat, there he was, patiently waiting for his goodies, which they all received a great deal of!

It's a family tradition to try and make opening presents on Christmas Day last all day; we had been doing a great job so far. Chief was crashed on the couch with the other guys almost the entire time. He went out or got up when he heard any one do the same, but he was in the middle of it for most of the day.

All of the animals at our house get presents for Christmas too. So when it was time for the horses to get their presents, we all headed outside. Chief was right there with us, right behind me, in fact, bumping my leg with his nose. Norman's present was a peppermint flavored rubber ball with a handle so he could grab it in his mouth and go nuts…which he preceded to do the moment I gave it to him. Chief thought it was amazing! Indian was out in the pasture with Norman trying to figure out what he was doing with this new toy. Chief stayed outside the fence with Cowboy and watched from the sidelines. Mama's present was a new shiny nameplate for her halter, and Homes had already gotten new goodies during the show season. All of the ponies were served a very special warm peppermint bran mash for Christmas dinner. After Cowboy had shown Chief just where to find the most perfectly aged horse manure and they had their fill, we all went back inside to continue with the festivities.

After some afternoon snacks (and more presents) it was the dogs turn to open their presents. Yes, I wrap them up in gift bags and let each dog try to pull them out of the bags…sometimes they humor me, other times they don't. Luckily, this was one of those times they humored me. I prefer to buy the toys that don't have stuffing but do have squeakers. The stuffing eventually comes out and it's bad enough they feel the need to eat the "skins" but I really don't think all that synthetic stuffing would be good for their digestive systems. Jager's presents are usually stolen by the

Beagles later, but he enjoys pulling them out of the bag and gumming them for awhile. Cowboy and Indian both pulled their toys out of the bags and nosed them around for awhile before deciding the couch looked more intriguing. Chief was not really sure what to make of this ritual. He put his nose in his bag, but the crinkling of the tissue paper startled him, so he backed up. I carefully pulled out the paper to reveal the huge gray, squeaky squirrel that was folded up inside. Not really being an experienced present opener, he just stood there wondering, I'm sure, why everyone was staring at him staring at this bag. I pulled the big squirrel part way out and let him look at it. I shook it around a bit and discovered that the tail made a crinkling noise very similar to the tissue paper. This time, however, the noise was attached to something fun. He gently bit at the tail and dragged it the rest of the way out of the bag. Success! Chief's first Christmas present, we all said our "aaahhhh"s and our "he's so cute"s. Chief then decided the couch was looking pretty good at this point, so up he went and piled on top of the two that were already up there.

The rest of the day proved very uneventful but incredibly fun. Chief was becoming more comfortable with everyone around and we were on day two of no accidents. The horses are not the only ones that get a special Christmas dinner, the dogs do too. So after a huge meal all four dogs and all five humans were ready to call it a night. We piled into bed for a wonderfully long uninterrupted night of sound sleep. Woo hoo!

Day 6

Chapter 16

Game On!

We were lucky enough to have Bert's famous chicken fried steak again for breakfast so the whole family joined at our house again. Chief had already been out to do morning chores, and patrol the fence line. He was still a bit jumpy in the house with all the people and noises going on but he was so much better than the day before. We sat down to eat to a perfectly behaved, begging Beagle at the table. All the dogs are well behaved beggars, but, for no experience Chief's manners were impeccable. When we were finished each dog got a plate to clean. Chief was still not convinced he liked this idea so Cowboy tried to show him how, again.

The day was spent outside putting Christmas presents together, doing chores and otherwise just enjoying the beautiful weather. I went out to fill water buckets in the pasture and all the dogs came out with me to explore. Chief followed me out to the outer field where there are many trees and shrubs to play in. All the horses were out enjoying the warm sunshine in the outer field. Mo is the one horse that is incredibly grumpy and aggressive towards the dogs, so when Chief began to wander in his direction, I tried to make sure I was paying close attention. Not close enough… from behind the trees I heard a horrible yelp and out came Chief favoring his front paw and whining. I ran over to him and caught sight of a very guilty looking Mo. I carried him to the lawn by the house (wow was he getting heavy) and did a thorough check of his leg and his foot. After deciding he was physically fine, just scared, we went inside for a snack. Luckily, this last experience with Mo made its mark on Chief; he was now much wearier of the horses and was now staying out of the pastures when the horses were nearby.

Indian and Chief really started to play today...I mean actually play. They got into a tug of war with one of the skins and Chief really surprised Indian by not letting go when Indian growled and pulled. Cowboy usually just lets go when Indian starts to pull, so when Chief didn't give it up, Indian froze for a second. In a moment, it was like a switch was flipped in Indian's head and it was "game on"! They both started to pull and growl and Indian was trying the famous "Beagle butt swing" on him. It is a maneuver we have observed in both of our Beagles where they face their opponent while swinging their butts into them for leverage or to knock them off balance. Chief was bigger than Indian when he got to us, but he had gained some serious weight since he had been with us, so he had some size advantage in the tug of war that was going on. It went on for a few minutes with tails wagging, when Indian actually gave up the skin! Once Chief realized he had the prize, he took off. Psycho circles all by himself. It didn't take long for Indian to join in and they were off, everywhere, all over the place. It was so great to watch Chief, just let go of all he had been through and be a dog. We couldn't help but just stand and watch them play.

We said good bye to Gwen and Rick later that afternoon and got ready to go to the neighbor's house for our annual Boxing Day dinner. This would be the first time Chief would actually be left alone. Luckily, he was so exhausted from his day that he had fallen asleep on the bed, watching the basketball game while we were getting ready. Bert and I were able to sneak out without disturbing any of the sleeping dogs. I was nervous about leaving him and told myself I would be home by eight o'clock even if the festivities weren't over. After great company, wonderful food, and lots of wine, we made our way home right at eight o'clock. We had left the bedroom light on and as we walked by the window we stopped to see what was going on. There was Chief, still sacked out on the bed in front of the T.V. He was extremely cute and it was difficult to stop watching him lay there all curled up on the bed When we got inside, all the dogs, including Chief met us at the door for the free for all! Tails wagging, licking, jumping, whining, the whole thing. I love coming home!

Day 7-12

Chapter 17

Anniversary

Wow! Chief's one week anniversary with us. He was a part of the family already and he was such a fast learner. His whole "being" had changed so much in such a short amount of time. We were still in disbelief that he had only been "liberated" a little over a month ago. Oh the difference a month makes! He had gained a ridiculous amount of weight and, after his first bath; his coat had lost the dull smelliness and taken on an incredible shine with the smell of sage. His face was now expressive, relaxed, and curious and that worried look hadn't reappeared. His demeanor was the most noticeable; he no longer skulked, spooked or cowered. Instead he completely owned it all! He trotted around wherever he went with purpose, he played with the other dogs and me (not Bert yet for some reason), he didn't eat everything in sight in the same sitting anymore and only briefly stopped at the bowls before he went outside. Chief was learning to come when he was called and his begging skills were something to behold.

I had been waiting anxiously to hear from Shannon to give her an update on his progress. Her ears must have been burning because the telephone rang that morning. She was shocked about the potty training and how easy it had been, I left out the exploding stomach story from his first night. She was happy to hear that all the dogs were getting along and when I shared some of the stories with her I could tell how happy she was. We decided we would wait until after the New Year for the home visit and all the official business to make him ours, even though he was ours in every way possible. I was really looking forward to the visit because I so wanted to show off how well he was doing and looking.

Chapter 18

Road Trip

Bert is an excellent gift giver, so today we needed to drive to town to pick up my Christmas present. A new front door. We decided to bring the pack so they could have a run at Galway Downs, the show ground where Bert does the majority of his work. Chief was still trying to figure out where his spot in the truck was so the trip "down the hill" involved some shifting, especially because I was taking up the entire front seat (where two Beagles would usually have been).

After everyone settled in, it was already time to go crazy. When the Beagles get within some sort of secret Beagle smell range of their destination, they completely loose it. They start to walk around on your lap, off your lap, up on the dashboard, on the arm rests, all the while whining and moaning in impatience. Once to the destination, Bert can't get the doors open fast enough to let them out.

Chief was not yet privy to this ritual and luckily slept through most of it. Bert let the hounds out to run while we stayed in the truck and drove out to the middle of the property. The dogs are really good about following the truck, or at least going in the general direction, but it makes me exceedingly nervous when they are right in front of the truck while Bert is driving, I usually have to close my eyes or look in another direction until we have gotten where we are going.

Chief stood on Bert's lap while he was driving with his nose at the open window, but he was definitely not ready for the head out the window with the tongue hanging out routine yet. We pulled up to a beautiful water complex that was unfortunately empty at the time but had some nice long green grass and mud. Chief was very much like Cowboy in that green grass was an open invitation to roll and relax. He wasn't really sure about the mud...I was pretty sure that would change after spending more time with Cowboy and Indian. Chief had a harness and leash on because I was so paranoid he would get away while following our unruly bunch off on a hunt.

Bert drove the truck down to another part of the property where he knew we could turn on the water and see what Chief would do. Jager loved to swim and play in the water, Cowboy was the first one in if it was hot and would occasionally swim, Indian would just get his feet wet to cool off but preferred not to go in much past his belly. We were about to see where the new guy fit into the scheme of things. While Bert drove, I walked Chief down to meet him. He still wasn't in very good shape and for December it was awfully hot so it didn't take long for him to run out of steam. By the time we reached Bert we were walking so slowly we were barely moving, we had stopped every few feet to pull the horrible stickers out of his feet, and he really didn't look impressed. A new nick name was coming to me...Chief Droopy Drawers. The other dogs had made their way down to meet us and were ready to play in the water that was now running into the stream.

To our surprise, Chief went right in. He walked right in the water and started trying to eat the grass that was growing at the bottom and drink at the same time. The water was shallow, it just barely went above his paws and he was just fine with it. Bert convinced me to take him off the leash, and promised to catch him if he bolted off anywhere. He trotted around and stayed fairly close but wasn't really interested in staying with the other dogs; he went off in his own direction. Bert and I both noticed that he seemed to get a certain distance away from us and he would slow down or start to make his own way back. Already he was making progress from that first day we had taken him out at home. He seemed to be on smell overload. His head just jerked around in this direction, then that direction his nose on the ground the entire time. There was only one instance when Bert actually did have to run after him, not because he bolted but because he just got too far away and kept on going.

After about an hour, sufficient time to get thoroughly dirty, we decided to load up and run our errands. It has always amazed me that Bert feels completely comfortable leaving his truck running with the air conditioning on for the dogs while he is inside. He always tells me that anyone brave enough to try and get in with Jager in there barking, snarling, and carrying on could have the truck. His philosophy had proven true so far, I was just wondering how much longer the ancient bird dog would be considered a deterrent! We were inside for about forty five minutes and when we returned all the puppies were peacefully sleeping in their spots. Chief was becoming more and more like one of the guys every day.

Chapter 19

Chief the Thief

Sleeping and the sleeping arrangements were no longer an issue; Chief was sleeping through the night and had actually started to enjoy sleeping in. His morning nickname had become Chief Lazy Bones. He and Cowboy were the last ones in bed with me even if Bert was up and outside doing chores. He was starting to utterly enjoy the creature comforts of his new home. He knew where to sit for cookies, where his dinner spot was, where to crash on the couch, where to sleep on the bed, where the fun things were to steal (my closet and Bert's bathroom), how and when to beg for people food, he had it all down to a science.

Today was the day for Bert to install my new door, luckily the weather was perfect so having the door open, or no door at all was not a problem. Chief the Thief was back in full force "helping" Bert with his tools, weather stripping, tool belts, boxes of screws (which I had to pick up as he ran across the property), and various other objects. He was still very scared of the loud noises from the nail gun and any banging that was going on, but was able to overcome his fear when he realized there was a lunch time snack inside.

Once the door was installed and the screen door was back up, we realized that the latch for the screen was gone so it just swung open on its own. The weather was so nice out I wanted to leave the new door open and let some fresh air in through the screen, Chief thought that was a great idea too!

He loved pushing the door open with his nose to go out then turning right around and opening the door with his paw to come back in. I don't think it would have gotten old for Chief...but I was tired of the door open and flies coming in, so I decided to put a door draft stopper on the outside of the door so he could no longer push it open. Chief wasn't impressed. A while later I realized the door was swinging open again so I just closed the front door, forgetting all about the door draft stopper. When I went out to feed later that afternoon there was my draft stopper, out by the trailer, covered in dirt, with a small hole in the end of it. Chief the Thief had struck again.

It was the end of another very positive day for the new guy. He had discovered that the delicacy of horse manure was available 24/7 and required no effort on his part to get. He was now completely potty trained, doggie door trained, truck trained, and on his way to be being horse trained. Dinnertime had become uneventful, until tonight. Indian was actually completely cleaning his bowl tonight so when Chief came by to check all the bowls, Indian started a low deep growl. We hadn't given Chief's lack of social skills much thought until he completely disregarded Indian's warning and pushed him off the bowl. Bert and I were both surprised that Indian let Chief bully him. Of all the dogs Indian is the "scrappiest" and definitely doesn't put up with a lot, so to see him just give in was not at all what we expected. We were both hoping this would be the one and only disagreement.

Chapter 20

Pecking Order

Chief was starting to fall into the routine of the ranch life, unfortunately I was going to be going back to work soon and so was Bert, but until then, we enjoyed our lives of leisure. Up early to feed horses and then usually back to bed for a cuddle, a morning snack then we would start the day. We were meeting Gwen and Rick at the show ground today to get a load of fire wood for both households. The majority of Bert's work involves carving and constructing obstacles for horses to jump over so he has access to a lot of wood scraps that we use during the winter to heat the house. However, it does need to be cut into manageable sized pieces and brought home. Rick and Gwen recently replaced their fireplace and wanted some wood to burn.

We decided to bring the pack with us; we took every chance to get Chief out and about. As soon as we got on the property, Bert let the hounds out of the truck to run. Chief was very brave this trip and put his paws up on the window and had his head almost all of the way out. He kept a close eye on Cowboy and Indian as they made their way down to the "bone yard" where all the old wood scraps and lots of bunnies could be found. I let him out when we reached our destination and was going to be brave myself by not putting on his leash. He ran around sniffing the piles of wood and debris, over and under, not really staying with the others, and certainly not worried about whether or not I could keep up with him.

While Bert and Rick used chainsaws to cut up the wood (Chief was completely oblivious to the noise) and my mom and Gwen chatted, I chased Chief around, stressing that he would find the huge hole in the fence and go right through it into the road. Sure enough...it was like a magnet. He went right to the hole; luckily I was nearby and was able to get to him before he went through. I put his leash back on and tried to get him and the other two to follow me down the fence line. Once we were a safer distance from the hole, I let him back off the leash to see what he would do. The magnetic rays of escape started pulling him, once again, towards the hole in the fence. I gave up worrying about him and put his leash back on. I persuaded him to go with me in another direction but Cowboy and Indian were used to having free reign and decided to go off in another direction.

At this time of year, the ground is covered with the most brutal stickers, the kind that sting when they stick you. Poor Chief with his tender feet was stopping every few yards holding up one paw or another with a huge sticker in it. After a short while, he had had enough and just stopped all forward movement and sat down. No amount of pulling or coaxing could make him budge, so I ended up carrying him back to the truck. He was not amused. New nick name Chief Tender Feet.

While we were waiting for the boys to finish up, my mom, Gwen and I were talking and standing with Jager and Chief. Occasionally, Jager "shorts out" and just starts barking and going after whoever happens to be close by. Cowboy will usually roll over on his back if it is directed at him, and Indian usually laughs at him and just runs away. This time it was Chief, and this time Chief wasn't going to put up with it. As soon as Jager moved toward him with his snarling almost toothless mouth open, Chief moved toward Jager with his snarling mouth open. It only took a second of that horrible high pitched dog fight sound for me to yank Chief by his leash off Jager, who had fallen down because he is so rickety. I believed it to be a harmless demonstration of the "pecking order" being figured out. There was never an issue with the other three because Cowboy and Indian were both introduced as puppies and respected Jager as the head honcho. Chief on the other hand wasn't well versed in dog dynamics and was still trying to figure out where his spot was in our little pack.

After all the wood was cut and loaded, we said our goodbyes and loaded the pack into the truck. Any problems between Jager and Chief had completely disappeared and they all sacked out in the truck for the ride home. The rest of the afternoon was uneventful and lazy.

Chapter 21

Pillow Fight

Happy New Year!

We all slept right through the ball dropping and all the other festivities, but woke up to a beautiful morning. Chief's morning routine was becoming apparent by this time and it was hilarious. Once he was finally out of bed, the fun began. He would race around the house, slipping and sliding on the wood floors, looking for a toy, a slipper, a sock, or anything else that would work to play with. He would always end up back up on the bed with something to rough house with. Today, he was on the bed; empty mouthed looking for something...the pillow. He grabbed Bert's pillow and started wrestling with it. The way he rolled around with the pillow made it look like the pillow had a life of its own. One minute he was on top, the next, the pillow had the upper hand; it was a battle on the bed. This lasted for a few minutes before he saw me watching him and he was out of breath, so he casually moved away from the pillow for a snooze.

It was now becoming a habit to throw all the dogs in the truck when we went anywhere. If the truck was already running, Chief was too afraid of the noise to get close so we would usually pick him up and put him in. If the truck was off, he would wait by the door, but he wasn't ready to jump in by himself yet. Bert was on his way to see a friend who had just bought a house in our neck of the woods. When they got back, Bert couldn't wait to tell me how well Chief had done at this unfamiliar place. The property was only cleared right around the house; the rest of it was the tall sage brush, trees, and a tangle of underbrush. When Bert opened the door of the truck, Cowboy, Indian, and Jager all took off into the underbrush for some hunting. Chief stayed right with Bert while they walked around the house, he never left his side, even while the others were off exploring. Bert was so proud of him...he was beaming.

Chief's wagging tail, happy face and bark were becoming a normal, everyday occurrence. He was joining in with the other dogs to run down to the fence and bark at passing cars or people. Chief the Thief visited almost every day, stealing clothes off the floor the slippers off my feet, and today tried to carry Bert's heavy work boot up onto the bed. He seemed to like shoes, every ones shoes. I found mine scattered around the house or sometimes outside, Bert's often ended up on the bed. My mom's were occasionally across the property, and regrettably chewed on. He hadn't chewed on any of our shoes but he had damaged a pair or two of my mom's. I was hoping this wasn't going to become a habit.

Chapter 22

A Dinner Party

We were having friends over for dinner tonight which would be a new challenge for Chief. It would be the most people he had been exposed to at one time, six, including us.

We had let our guests know, ahead of time, all about the new guy and what he was worried about. All of them, being dog people, were very respectful of our requests to keep things low key.

When they arrived, he skulked around for a short while, but as soon as everyone settled in, sat down and started chatting he made his way around to everyone saying hi and getting pet. He did spend the majority of the evening outside, even when we sat down for dinner and the others were inside looking for a goodie, Chief kept his distance. He finally joined us inside when our guests were heading out and I was cleaning up the kitchen, this was a quieter opportunity for goodies.

As soon as the house was quiet again, he was himself again. We loved that the worried face never came back and he wasn't afraid of all the new people. More and more progress every day.

Chapter 23

What If...

This morning was special because instead of staying down at the foot of the bed while we were sleeping in, Chief crept up to my head on his belly with his front paws out in front of him, laid his head on my pillow right next to my face, and fell asleep. I couldn't possibly get up with this adorable Beagle lying next to me like this. Not to mention, my two week vacation was almost over and I wanted to be a bum for just a few more mornings. Chief was so cute I didn't want to disturb him by moving away from him…but his breath was horribly bad.

Cowboy has never had a bad breath issue, Indian's breath is pretty bad, and Jager's is so bad it is indescribable. Chief's was right up there between Indian's and Jager's, not good. Shannon had shared with us that many of the rescue Beagles had rotten teeth that needed to be pulled and that many of them may have had chemicals poured down their throats. In the laboratories these dogs were only ever fed small amounts of soft food that they were expected to lick from between the bars of their cages. Chief actually had good looking teeth, but his breath could very well have been a result of chemicals, it was impossible to tell, all I knew was he was cuddled up next to me with his head on my pillow like he had been with me since he was a puppy. No amount of bad breath could make me move at this point. New nick name Chief Halitosis.

After a morning snack, we went out to the field across the street for a walk in the wilds. I let the other three dogs go but kept Chief on his leash. I noticed he was starting to become interested and run toward Cows and Indian when they sounded off because of a scent. He wasn't sure what to do once he got there, but he was paying closer attention to what they were doing. I tried to let him off the leash for a while and luckily he wasn't very interested in blazing trails through the underbrush so he was easy to keep an eye on. At one point, a rabbit ran across his path and he actually took off after it. It took only seconds for him to be too far away for me to grab him. Fear gripped me as all the horrible "what ifs" flew through my mind. What if...I can't catch him? What if...he runs into the road? What if...I have to call Shannon to tell her he's gone? While my mind raced, so did my feet! I called his name over and over until he actually slowed down enough for me to gain some ground. He never stopped completely but he slowed down enough so I could catch him by his harness. Wow! He had scared me to death, but all I could do was hug and squeeze him, which probably was not the best training technique to use for a dog that won't come when he is called...but that was not my concern at the moment. That was it, all the off leash training would have to be done by Bert. My nerves just couldn't handle it.

When we got back to the house, Cows and Indian were still out rampaging so I closed the gate. I stayed out front with Chief and Jager so we could let them in when they finally returned. In the meantime, I got some duck jerky (a favorite new treat) to work on some "comes" with Chief. He is very food motivated so the practice went quite well until he figured out I had a bunch in my hand so he just kept coming. I certainly do not fancy myself a dog trainer, but I was hoping this little lesson would help.

Chapter 24

New Experiences

Once the whole pack was back in the yard, locked up tight, it was time to exercise the horses. Chief was getting much better around the horses and would now wait by the trailer door for apple cookies even if one of the horses was tied there. When we weren't trail riding, I would exercise the horses in our arena at the front of the property and the dogs would usually follow me out there and either sunbathe in the dirt or explore. I rode Homes first, and the moment I got on, Chief took off. He spent the forty minutes I was riding Homes over at my mom's hanging out with her. When I put Homes away and got Mama out, Chief caught sight of me and joined all of us at the trailer again for cookies. This time, when I got on Mama, Chief stayed nearby and trotted out to the arena behind us with Indian. Progress. I was hoping if he would get used to following me while I was on horseback he would be able to trail ride with us soon. Chief didn't stay out in the arena with us, as soon as I did more than walk he took off back towards the trailer. When I was finished working Mama and walked her back to the trailer, Chief was waiting by the door, he started to run away when we got closer, but I called his name and he looked thoroughly confused, like he recognized the voice but not me (with my helmet on, I wouldn't recognize me either). When I got off, took off my helmet and called to him again, he ran over to me, jumped up and was very happy to see me. Of course, all the dogs had to join in, and Indian always has to give the horses kisses too.

After the horses were put away and the dogs, once again, had my undivided attention we got down to some serious playing. Chief and Indian got into a great game of tug of war with Cowboy's favorite raccoon skin, so he was on the sidelines barking and jumping around. Once Indian grabbed the skin and took off, the "psycho circles" began. Chief's stamina was increasing everyday so he was able to keep up with Indian (also known as "the cheetah") for a while longer than he had before. They ran everywhere, in and out of the trees, around the trailer, on and off of the deck, under chairs and tables; it was great to watch the two of them together. All I could think about, watching Chief running in circles was him sitting in that tiny crate for five years never running and never playing. I was so happy for him. Cowboy has his own version of psycho circles too, which I think is pretty smart. Instead of following the others around and around, he finds a place to sit that is right in their path and just barks and lunges at them every time they pass by. Very effective with not a lot of energy expended. That's Cowboy's motto.

Today was the last day of my winter break. It was going to be so hard to go back to work, not only because for the first time in eleven years of teaching, I wasn't enjoying my job, but because of the new guy and everything I would miss.

Day 13-16

Chapter 25

Nothing Is Off Limits

Great progress was made during the night, Chief got up during the night on his own, got a drink and went outside…all by himself. I made sure I paid attention to all the noises he made and was ready to get up if the noises stopped but when I heard the doggie door; I knew we were over any potty training issues. He came back in, checked all the bowls for leftovers, and hopped back up onto the bed. New nick name, Chief I Got This, my little boy was growing up.

None of us wanted to get up today. Chief was all curled up at Bert's feet, Indian was up on the pillows between us and Cow's was under the covers at my side. Even Jager was still snoring on his sheep skin. The only thing that made me feel remotely better about leaving Chief home, was that Bert would be there working for a few more days so he wouldn't be alone. He made it difficult to get ready to go, as every time I laid something out to wear, he would take off with it. My pants, my shoes, my underwear…nothing was off limits, it was everywhere. He went from being experimented on to experimenting with everything possible to make me late.

I had to have Bert lock everyone in the house so I could l leave. Bert's next project was to build a fence that went from the house to the property fence so we could lock everyone in the "backyard". The three dogs were actually pretty good about staying when someone was driving out of the gate. Chief on the other hand hadn't gotten that memo yet and the last thing I wanted was to have him slip out of the gate when someone was going through it.

After a horribly long day at school I drove up to our gate and was welcomed by three barking, baying Beagles. Chief was one of the guys. My mom held onto Chief so I could get in the gate, I opened my truck door and Indian and Cows both jumped in for the short ride up the driveway. When I got out of the truck I was mauled by the three Beagles. It was funny how much I had missed spending time with all of them. I have to stop from time to time and realize how great my life is and how much I love all those that are in it, this was one of those times. After kisses and hugs, I had to get the recap of the day.

Chapter 26

Not Enough Hands

My mom has really become a huge help on the property with chores and general animal care. She feeds lunch to the horses and cleans and fills water buckets and takes puppy patrol for the day. Because this is all a fairly normal routine, I didn't think there would be that much of a change by adding one more Beagle to the equation. I was wrong.

The day started for my mom cleaning water buckets, Bert had gone to run some errands without the dogs and she was waiting for a feed delivery. Busy, busy, busy. Of course, everything that could've happened did, all at once. While cleaning one of the water buckets, she found an owl that had drowned in it the night before. While trying to get it out, the feed truck pulled up and was waiting at the gate. She went to grab a hold of Chief's collar so she could open the gate and as she did; he got out of his collar, ran for the opening gate and slipped out. Drowned owl in one hand, watching Chief run out as the feed truck came in… it was too much! Mom dropped the owl, closed the gate so the rest of the pack wouldn't get out and took off after Chief. Luckily, he came when she called him in an excited high pitched voice and made a huge deal out of him when he got to her. Crisis averted.

Chapter 27

The Front Lawn

Things had settled down by the time I got home and it was time to exercise horses. Chief followed me everywhere. Even though Bert was home working on the new fence, Chief was with me nudging my leg reminding me he was there. He played with Indian and was becoming an expert at "psycho circles" and I had caught him trying the old Beagle butt swing on his playmate.

He was becoming much braver about the horses and would come and "hang out" with me by the trailer while I was getting the horses ready. Although I believe the apple treats inside the trailer played a very large role in him overcoming his fear, either way, he was improving and learning how to respect the horse's space. Today I was doing ground work with the horses, which meant I was on the ground working the horses around me in a circle. Chief followed me out to the arena and actually sat next to me in the center of the circle; he watched the horses and followed me if I moved. At one point, he saw Indian take off after something and jumped to go with him, luckily Mama was paying attention and between the two of us were able to avoid running him over. Still not completely aware of the damage a horse could do to his little body but getting better!

After the horses were all tucked in and the afternoon was winding down, we all went to the front lawn for some fun. This is when and where the "psycho circles" began, where we wrestled, played tug of war, and just generally had fun. This is also when Jager sometimes joined in, he couldn't do much but he tried, in his own unstable way, to play. Cowboy was still intimidated by him and would usually just roll over, Indian would play with him but his craziness usually proved too much for the old guy. Now there was Chief, who still didn't quite understand Jager's personality. One bark led to another and in a moment they were fighting again. I don't think you could actually call it a fight, Chief lunged at Jager and Jager fell down, barking and snarling the entire time. The thing that I didn't necessarily like, or understand was that each time it had happened, Chief erred on the side of aggression, not submission.

Chapter 28

Old Dog...New Tricks

Another day at work that Chief made very difficult to get ready for. Besides being so cute and cuddly he was in the habit now of stealing whatever I put down. He was very wound up in the morning and ran around the bedroom picking up toys, jumping on the bed to wrestle with them or running across the wood floor after something and sliding for miles throughout the house. It was so much fun to watch that I would lose track of time and end up late.

Jager and Chief had another run in before I left for work, while Chief was playing with Indian. Again, Chief didn't back down and poor Jager fell down. Would Jager be the one to figure this one out? Would this be a trick an old dog could learn? Don't pick on the new guy. This time Chief walked around Jager with his hackles up for a few moments until they heard Bert go out the door. The trance was broken, all was forgiven and everyone went outside. This pattern of behavior was starting to worry me, me only though. Bert didn't seem bothered at all by Chief's behavior and wrote it off to being new and completely socially inept. When he reminded me that poor Chief had been in a cage, isolated for five years with no contact with other dogs...I felt much better that all wasn't perfect in "Beagle Land". I found I was taking it personally that the dogs weren't getting along perfectly, but in reality...it had nothing to do with me and they were getting along really well considering all the changes they were all experiencing.

I found work to be very depressing and it was difficult to get through each day without thinking about everything I had waiting for me at home. I was teaching a subject I was not qualified to teach at a grade level I was not qualified nor interested in teaching, to a group of kids that couldn't have cared less about what they were being taught. I started to realize, the moment I left the house, that deep, scowly, mad wrinkle between my eyebrows carved its way in before I even got to school. My eyebrows were fully functional just like Chiefs. A very compassionate, animal loving, coworker pointed out to me that I needed something good at home to cancel out all the bad that was going on at work...I did have something, I had lots of things. I had to hold all my positives close and remind myself of them all the time. Chief and all his progress, my great husband, my wonderful dogs, my talented loving horses, my amazing mother...Once I realized how long the list really was, it really did cancel out the one negative, work. Even though I spent the majority of my day at work, I was lucky enough to spend the rest of my time with all my positives. Funny how rescuing a helpless little Beagle from Spain was completely transforming my way of thinking, and living for that matter.

Chapter 29

Another Great Day

When I got home, Bert was working on the new fence for the backyard. All the dogs were outside running around and met me at the gate when I got there…instant smile on my face! When I opened the gate, Chief ran away because of the noise from my truck, Cows and Indian jumped in the door, and Jager was up with Dad (Bert's nickname). As soon as I got far enough in the gate to close it, Chief slipped out. I luckily just caught sight of him in the rearview mirror, so I was able to jump out and call him before he got to too far away. I was so happy that he actually came when I called him and followed me in gate that my horrible day was erased from my memory.

Bert told me all about the day and how much Chief "helped" him with the fence. Helped himself to all of his tools was more like it! Bert was laughing as he told me about how funny it was to watch him try and drag the hammer away without being noticed. Or how much time he wasted looking for all the things that had been mysteriously removed from their spots. Bert was trying his best to look annoyed but it wasn't working at all.

Then he told me about the fantastic tug of war he was able to catch between Chief and Indian. Indian was still surprised when his opponent wouldn't let go when he started tugging. By this time Chief had about fifteen pounds on Indian (note to self…time to cut back on the chow!) so the one being tugged around was Indian, he wasn't really happy about this, and his snarling was louder than ever, as was Chief's. Bert said the tails were wagging furiously and they looked like they were having so much fun. Chief was literally dragging Indian across the lawn! At one moment, Chief stopped to get a better grip on the squirrel skin, Indian saw his opportunity for victory and in the split second Chief opened his mouth to reposition; Indian snatched the squirrel from his mouth and took off. Bert said the gait in which he took off was like nothing he had ever seen. It was a cross between his fast cheetah pace and a victorious bunny hop. I was getting as much enjoyment from the story as I was from watching Bert retell it.

That night we were getting ready to pile into bed, when I remembered, the best way to get a good spot was to be the first one in. I snuggled in and was joined quickly by Shmin who curled up with me on the pillows in his "spot". Next was Cows, who laid down right in the center of the bed (sorry Bert) and made himself as big as possible. Then came Chief, who decided he wanted Indian's spot tonight. We call it "the dark face" when Indian gets mad. His eyes dilate, his face wrinkles up, and his face actually looks darker. As Chief approached us to muscle in on our cuddle, Indian put on his dark face and started a low, deep growl. I was a little worried about how this was going to play out, only because of what had already transpired between him and Jager. To my surprise and sheer happiness, Chief walked away calmly and lay down next to Cowboy. Woo hoo! I think he's learning what all this dog stuff is about! Indian settled right down and

Bert wedged himself in between Beagles to join us in bed. Another great dog day was over.

Day 17-21

Chapter 30

Home Alone

Today was going to be a landmark day for Chief. Today would be the first day he would be alone, both Bert and I were going to work today. My mom would be home…but I hated leaving her with that responsibility. I had convinced Bert to leave the other dogs home so Chief wouldn't feel completely abandon and would have company. The new fence was finished, but missing one board, so we were hoping it would hold him in long enough for us to get out the gate safely.

It was time to get up…I got up while Bert and the puppies stayed in bed for a while longer. When I looked back at the bed, Chief was curled up next to Bert with his head on his pillow. Next to Chief was Indian who was all curled up between our pillows, buried in the blankets. At the foot of the bed was a big round lump under the quilt…Cowboy. It took all my will power not to just climb back in bed to cuddle with my boys, knowing both Bert and I were leaving, made it all the harder.

We spent the morning playing with toys and doing chores. He nudged me constantly while we were walking around to feed the horses. I think he knew things were going to be different today; he stayed very close all morning. He kept grabbing my skirt and pulling on it while I was trying to get dressed, my shoes, my stockings, he even jumped up and stole my brush off the counter. Chief the Thief was in rare form this morning. If his plan was to make me feel awful about leaving him...it was working. I purposefully left first, so all the dogs could all look at Bert with those "please don't leave us" faces on. I found it cruel and unusual punishment to say good bye to the dogs for the day, especially when I had to go to work and tough it out at a job I did not enjoy.

When I got home, I got the day's recap before I even got out of the truck. Bert locked them in the new backyard and headed out without any problems. However, not long after Bert left, Chief was sitting on my mom's doorstep scratching at the door. The little smarty found the hole in the fence and hopped right through it. None of the other dogs did it, just him. New nickname, Chief Escape Artist.

My mom has a great little cat named Sock that lives inside only. She is very careful about doors when she leaves and we have been very lucky to catch him right away the few times he has escaped. So, today when she went out to feed lunch to the horses she didn't worry about whether or not the door was closed. Something, when she was telling me the story later she couldn't remember what it was, made her turn around to go back to the house. When she did, she realized the door was open. She quickly went in to find Sock, and instead found Chief taking the five cent tour all on his own. He trotted right by Sock a few times and paid absolutely no attention to him, like he wasn't even there. That was great news because the others get a little "excited" around cats. I was finding there might be a bonus or two to living in a cage for his whole life... no idea what cats were or how to react to them. She didn't even have to call him; he trotted right out the door on his own and headed outside.

For the first day being left alone, the day was very uneventful. I was relieved to hear that not much had happened. My mom told me that he spent the majority of the day outside with Indian just hanging around. They were locked in the backyard when I pulled in and as soon as they heard the truck pull up they went nuts. I could barely get the gate open as they were all up against it barking and whining. When I finally did, the mauling began, so happy to be home!

Chapter 31

Off To Work

Another landmark day for the new guy…his first day at work with Bert!

We woke up to Chief cuddled up with Indian in the pillows. So cute. As soon as we got up, everyone was off and running. Bert went out to do chores and all the puppies went out with him. I couldn't believe it…Chief had just left the building without eating first. It was a first. He checked all the bowls when he came back in so I gave him a little snack…it was going to be a big day for the little guy.

He was so wound up this morning, more so than usual. I was really starting to believe that he knew when something was going on and whether it was good or bad. At one point he jumped up on the bed, grabbed Bert's pillow and started wrestling so hard with it that he hooked the corner of a fairly large painting above the bed and pulled it off the wall. The noise and the action of the painting sliding down the wall behind the bed scared him enough to make him jump off the bed. As soon as I came in the room, started laughing, and put the painting back up, he was right back on the bed playing with the pillow. The progress was staggering at times. We started finding ourselves saying things like, "he would've never done that before", or "can you imagine what he would have done a few weeks ago?" We wouldn't think about every little thing he did as often but when something happened that warranted some kind of reaction on his part and the reaction was positive, it was very obvious how much he was changing.

When Bert was about to leave and all the dogs came running into the bedroom, all of a sudden Chief and Indian were at each other. I had no idea what or why this was happening, all I knew was that neither one of them was really backing down and the sound was horrific. Just as quickly as it had started, it stopped. Cowboy was panicking and looked incredibly worried so as soon as I hugged him for reassurance, I checked Indian over; he was missing a microscopic amount of hair above his eye. Then to Chief…he was fine. However, the entire time I was tending to the Beagles, Chief was walking in circles around Indian with his hackles up growling, at one point he tried to put his head over Indian's back (I had learned along the way that this was a sign of dominance). It all really did happen rather quickly so when Bert just shouted "let's go!" all seemed to be forgotten and they all followed him out to the truck.

STRESS! I needed all to be well in Beagle land. Chief and Indian had been getting along swimmingly so this was a real surprise. Once again, Bert told me not to worry about it; they would work it out themselves. He loaded everyone in the truck, and while he was putting Jager in the backseat…Chief jumped into the front seat, all by himself. He must have really wanted to go because this was the first time he had done this on his own. The plan for the day involved my mom picking Chief up from the show ground at noon, so he would be there only half the day in case things weren't going well. Wow! All this for her grand dogs, what would we have done without her?

Chapter 32

First Day on the Job

All I can say here is…ignorance is bliss! I was so glad Bert was doing this and not me. He started off the day turning Chief loose to see what he would do. Right away he followed Cowboy and Indian across the street. As soon as he got there, a huge truck drove by and scared him to death! He bolted away, not far luckily, and hid under a bush. Bert was close enough and had his eye on him the whole time so he was able to go and calm him down and bring him back to where he was working. Poor Chief was very obviously not ready to be left on his own.

Next on Bert's list of things to try was to tie him to Jager. It didn't really go as well as when the two puppies had been tied to him in the past, after all that was almost four years ago when Jager was in much better shape. Now we were hoping the nineteen year old bird dog with nonexistent hip joints could handle the five year old "puppy" with no social skills or life experience. Bert took the loop of a leash and tied it around Jager's collar and snapped the other end to Chief's harness. Chief would take off at his purposeful trot in a direction and poor Jager was just dragged along for the ride. And so went the rest of the morning. Poor Jager put up with the ride until my mom arrived to pick up Chief.

The ride home was another adventure all together. My wonderful mother ended up taking all of the Beagles home instead of just Chief. Chief has become a very good passenger but he has only ever ridden in trucks that have a bench seat in the front and the gear shift on the steering column. Well...my mom's car is not put together that way. Instead, her gear shift, parking brake and window operation buttons are on a console between the front seats. This is where Chief decided he would sit for the ride home because Indian was in the front seat and wasn't about to budge and Cows was spread out across the entire backseat. Needless to say the ride home involved windows going up and down, Chief trying to balance on either side of the parking brake and at one point, the car "slipping" out of gear. Gale is a patient woman and a calm driver so she made it home in one piece, but after hearing the story that afternoon, I was quite sure she wouldn't want to play taxi driver again.

Chapter 33

The Scrap

Bert was already home when I arrived from work. Among all of the other things he is capable of doing; Bert takes care of our horse's feet as well. He trims and put shoes on all of the horses that live at our house. This is a great treat for the dogs because, for whatever reason, they love to eat the pieces of hoof that are trimmed off. I have discovered, over the years that dogs find enjoyment in some of the strangest delicacies, most of which, I will never understand.

Mo is the only one that does not have shoes so the pieces of hoof that Bert trims off are nice and thick and perfect for the dogs. Indian grabbed a perfect piece and settled down under a tree for a great chew, the kind where his eyes roll back in his head, the muscle in the top of his head bulges up and down as he chews and he becomes entranced and oblivious. Chief, who had yet to experience this culinary delight, was just sitting back, watching the commotion. Watching...until he realized how happy Shmin was with his hoof cookie (that's what they are called at our house). So, he decided that he wanted that hoof cookie and paid absolutely no attention to Shmin's warning growl and up turned lip...the dark face. Then came the scrap. Indian and Chief were going at it and it didn't seem that either one was going to stop! I was holding Norman for Bert, who was under him trying to get his shoe nailed on. We both froze for a moment...then climbed through the fence to stop the fracas.

Bert grabbed Indian by the scruff and lifted him off the ground and our rushing up to the situation was enough to snap Chief out of his trance. Poor Cowboy was a mess. The entire time they were going at it, Cows was inches away barking and jumping up and down as if he was yelling "Stop it you guys! Please...can't we just be friends?" I think he was more traumatized by this then the other two were. They had just walked away from each other after we checked them all over for wounds and moved on. I made sure to find the hoof cookie that was the root of this disagreement and dispose of it.

Cows needed some serious hugs before we could continue with Norman who luckily just stood there with his shoe only half way nailed on. I was a mess. "We need to call Cesar Milan, we need some Dog Whispering!" I told Bert. I was glad he didn't write my concern off as just being emotional this time. We talked about it and he thought it was still pecking order being established, he felt that it could have been a much more serious fight if it was really an aggressiveness problem. Neither dog had any injuries and it seemed to have been more vocal than physical. These were all valid points and as he was making them...the two of them were chasing each other around with tails up and wagging! Okay, I'll wait to call the Dog Whisperer, I thought. Everyone was great for the rest of the evening and Chief was exhausted from his day with Bert. He sacked out on the couch after dinner and didn't move again until we went into the bedroom for bed. Whew!

Chapter 34

Good Ole Cowboy

This would be Chief's second day with Bert. He already knew in the morning that he wanted to go and followed us both around everywhere we went so he wouldn't get left behind. He would still only hop in the truck on his own if it wasn't running, and because the mornings had been so cold, Bert would start the truck a while before he was ready to go so it would warm up. This meant lifting all of the dogs, except Indian, into their spots in the truck. Cowboy managed to tear both of his ACL's a while ago and we have only fixed one of them. The surgery involves an extensive, expensive procedure and quite a bit of layup time. He has been doing well on the one that hasn't been fixed but he doesn't like to jump up into the truck anymore. So the little jumping bean, also known as Indian, is the only one that will jump right into the truck when it is time to go. Or should I say, he jumps right in when he isn't pouting for one reason or another or flopping down on the ground like a rag doll so you have to pick him up too. It's always an adventure to try and go anywhere so many moods and personalities to try and wrangle.

Bert's approach today would be to try Cowboy and Chief together. Cowboy, the best dog in the world, would hopefully be a better match for Chief than Jager was. He weighs in at a solid fifty pounds (plus or minus depending on the time of year!) so it would be much harder for Chief to just drag him around. He is also incredibly obedient so he would be a good teacher for the new guy.

Bert's report that afternoon was very positive. When Bert first gets down to the property, he lets the dogs out for a quick lap around the perimeter. Today would be Chief's first try. Bert opened the truck door and the hounds took off. Chief started off with them until Bert started to drive off in the truck, then he just sat down and watched him drive away. Bert stopped, went back and picked him up. I think he's going to need a little bit more time before he catches on to this ritual.

Cowboy led Chief around all day; however, they never went very far. Cowboy knew this was not going to be a good hunting day so he never wandered off to the good hunting spots. Every time Bert called for them, Cowboy would drag Chief, sometimes unwillingly, back to where he was waiting for them. Cows was a great teacher but did his best to look and act incredibly put out by his new job. Cowboy is famous for his expressions, he has many. The one he wore today we call "the long face", he does an incredible job of making his whole face look longer than normal, like he has a mile long frown on his face. The moment Bert disconnected them…Cows was ready to go, when he realized it was time to get in the truck and go home…he was not amused; "long face" all the way home.

Chapter 35

Host with the Most

That night we had some visitors over for dinner, four people and three dogs. When our guests arrived it was still light enough to go out and visit the horses. All of the dogs joined us outside; while we were chatting we noticed that Chief was taking his new visitors on his own tour. It was the greatest thing; there he was leading three dogs down a path toward the arena. He would stop occasionally to let everyone catch up, and then he would continue. Of course, all of us being the kind of dog people that have conversations for our dogs, thought it was going something like this; "This is my new house and I live here with my new family and out here is a lot of things to smell and look at and I am having so much fun here and over here is where the rabbits are, I used to live in a cage you know..." All of this with a thick Spanish accent, very much like that of Antonio Banderas! They trotted around the property for a while longer then joined us inside.

Chief proved to be a very welcoming host. He was used to having human visitors but this was the first time we had canine visitors as well. He was not territorial at all and didn't worry about his food dish once. Instead he tried to get the other dogs to play and go outside with him! Eventually he even got on the couch and crashed. This was one of those moments Bert and I had to stop and marvel at the continued leaps and bounds this dog that had spent so much time in a cage was making. We were dying to get Shannon and Jean out to do our home visit so we could show off our fat, happy, well-adjusted laboratory beagle.

Chapter 36

Rituals

Day three with Bert!

When they got down to the property, Bert tried the ritual again. The hounds took off in front of the truck, Chief didn't go with the others, and instead, he followed the truck. Bert was beginning to get excited when all of a sudden Chief was distracted by something far more interesting and took off in another direction. Luckily the other dogs know the route so Bert was able to stop the truck and go get the wayward beagle...new name "Chief Oh Look a Chicken"!

After finally collecting the herd, Bert tied Chief to Cowboy and tried to get to work. Cows was absolutely not having it today. He sat his fifty pounds down by the truck and was not going to move. Chief tried, tried hard, but he was no match for fifty pounds of pouting beagle and they went nowhere. Bert never even bothered to try the Chief/Indian combination...that would be a disaster waiting to happen. First of all, Indian only weighs in at a mere twenty eight, pounds so Chief, who was continually growing more rotund every day, would drag him around wherever he wanted. Second, Indian is completely on his own schedule, he comes back when he is ready and usually not until then...not something I really wanted Chief to emulate. Indian has been a blast to have, very different from Cowboy (the most perfect dog in the world), and he is the spunky, independent one. It proved to be a very uneventful day and Bert finally got some work done.

These good, long, adventurous days made the evenings at home fairly quiet. Dinnertime for the dogs was going really well. Chief was learning to sit and wait for his bowl, however I still had to supervise just in case one of the others didn't finish and I had to put the bowl up so Chief wouldn't clean it up. New nickname Chiefy Beefy. He was my shadow in the kitchen every night while I was making dinner, usually asleep or close to it. He would join us at the table for dinner and was maintaining his impeccable table manners. Plate licking was now a talent and he enjoyed it quite a bit. His spot on the bed was a work in progress and he never really stayed in the same spot all night. When the other dogs took off howling at one sound or another, he was right there with them. He hadn't become the instigator yet, but I think it won't be long before he's the one that gets all the other guys going! Most mornings he was snuggled up to either Bert or me with his head on a pillow, just snoring away! The other dogs were becoming more and more tolerant of his lack of social skills and actually seemed to enjoy his invasion of their space (which looked like cuddling to me).

Chapter 37

Freedom

Day four with Bert!

Another adventure for Chief today! When they got down to the property and everyone was let out of the truck, he actually followed! Jager was no longer the first one, instead he meandered behind the truck and got to his destination on his own time, Chief chose this routine instead of running off with the other two beagles at top speed. Chief was improving every day; he was now following the truck on his own each morning.

Bert was working in a different place on the property today, one that would make keeping an eye on Chief much easier. The tactic today would be…complete freedom! Chief was on his own today. Bert did have a plan though…Puperoni! Every time Bert would call Chief and he would come back, he would get a piece of Puperoni. He was incredibly food motivated, which in this case, was working to our advantage. Bert found that he would wander around but stay fairly close for a few hours then come back to the truck, get in, and take a nap, a while later he would get up, and go back out.

This particular day he wandered off on his own for a bit and when he came back, Bert discovered he had found his first super smelly, possibly dead, thing to roll in. He was an official beagle! Unfortunately, we have discovered that beagles love to roll in the oldest, most rotten, stinky, decaying, dead things they can find, the smellier the better. Chief had discovered this trait (I was hoping this would be the one beagle thing he wouldn't pick up) and done a great job at his first try.

This was also the day that Chief discovered that his friends from our dinner party lived down on the property and went on daily runs with their person, Rick. As they ran by, Chief recognized his canine buddies and decided to go along for a jog. This first outing didn't work out well, Bert called; Chief kept jogging. Finally, Rick had to turn around and bring back our beagle. Bert had to hold onto him for the next few minutes until all his buddies were out of sight. Luckily, out of sight, out of mind. He stuck around on his own for the most of the afternoon. However, at one point, he decided to follow Cowboy and Indian to their favorite hunting spot, which happens to be under the fence on the other side of the road in a big field. It had been a short while since Bert had seen Chief, so he walked up over a berm where he could see quite a bit of the surrounding area. There they were…Cowboy and Indian trotting off towards the road with Chief not far behind. Not wanting to lose him completely, which is what would've happened if they had kept on going; Bert called all three of their names. To his complete surprise…the only one that stopped, turned around, and actually started heading back was Chief. He came all the way back on his own. The not so surprising part was that Cows and Indian just kept going. Bert made a huge deal out of him and filled him with Puperoni. When he was telling me about this later he said, "I think he's starting to understand English!"

Bert loaded all the pooches in the truck at the end of the day…even the extremely stinky one, and headed home. The travelling arrangements in the truck had finally settled down. Chief had been sitting on Bert's lap for the drive home, but he had become so heavy (there was so much more Chief to love now) and trying to get himself comfortable on Bert's lap had become impossible so he moved to the back with Jager. He had become a great traveler, and would just fall asleep as soon as the truck started to move. Sometimes Chief, Jager, and Cowboy would pile into the back together and no one would mind when Chief just laid on top of, in between, under, or over them.

When they got home…Chief went immediately into the bathtub. He was really good every time I bathed him; he just put his head down, his tail down, and waited for it all to be over. This time when he jumped out of the tub and I approached him with the towel, he went berserk! His tail was up and wagging he was howling at me and doing donuts around the bathroom, I could hear Indian outside whining and scratching at the door…he wanted in on the action. As soon as I opened the door, Chief tried to run out at the same time Indian tried to run in and they both ended up in a pile on the floor. In a split second they were up chasing each other throughout the house, Chief was slipping and sliding on the wood floor because I never did get to dry him off and Indian was just egging him on.

It was just another evening in a house full of crazy dogs.

Chapter 38

Mud Bath

We were still waiting to have our home visit from Shannon and Jean at the Beagle Freedom Project. I was starting to worry that maybe they weren't going to be able to come because of the distance. But today was our lucky day, I had gotten a call from Jean and we set up a Monday afternoon for her to come and visit. I was very excited. We would finally be able to show him off. But today was another day with Bert at work.

Things were going much more smoothly with all the routines at work. Chief would get out of the truck and follow it around the property with Jager. We were experiencing a ridiculous hot spell in January and Chief had figured out where the closest water complex was in relation to where Bert was working (we call it the Shamu water because Bert carved a Killer Whale as a jump and it is in the middle of this water complex) and would go down, sit in the water to cool off, and return to Bert all on his own, dropping to roll in the dirt on the way. He had learned the trick of getting in the truck to take his naps…usually right after he had cooled off in the Shamu water and was covered in mud! New nickname "Chief Muddy Feet". He had also discovered where the stash of Puperoni was kept and helped himself to the entire bag. Bert was quite impressed that he had actually managed to open the glove box to find them. His nose was obviously fully operational by now and he wasn't afraid to follow it.

It was about 2:30 in the afternoon when I got a text from Bert that simply said, "He came back". Of course being the complete panic-er and protective mother that I am, my mind raced with hundreds of horrible scenarios. Chief had been missing for hours and he only now made it back or Bert didn't even know he was missing and he just came back, or any number of stories involving Chief being lost and finally found. I immediately tried to text him to find out what was going on. I got no response. I tried calling…voice mail. I repeated this for another hour until Bert finally answered the phone. He could tell by my "tone" that I was worried so he told me the whole story… Rick came by for his morning run with all the dogs, as usual; Chief decided he wanted to join them. He and Jager took off down the road after Rick and his pack. When Bert realized they were getting a bit too far away, he called for Chief. Again, to his surprise, Chief stopped, turned around and came back all on his own.

When I got the full story I sighed with relief and told Bert about all the horrible thoughts that had gone through my mind. He was disappointed that Chief had already eaten his supply of Puperoni because he didn't have anything to reward him with for coming back. Chief had another great day with Bert and an equally good night at home.

Chapter 39

Not Impressed

The next few days, for one reason or another, Bert wasn't able to bring the dogs with him to work. Not that staying home on five acres should be a "bummer" for most dogs, but for ours…that was a different story. Ohhhh, the faces when it was time for me to leave! Bert got off easy in the mornings because he got to leave first, he wasn't the one that had to lock them behind the fence and listen to the whining and barking, and see the mile long faces staring at you as you left, it was brutal. So as I was pulling out down to the gate I was surprised to see Chief following my truck down the driveway. Like I said, they were supposedly locked behind the fence. My mom to the rescue again. She was apparently watching me leave through her window and saw Chief. She came out to hold on to him so I could leave, we would have to figure out how Chief Houdini had escaped when I got home.

When I returned later that afternoon, my mom showed me how he had managed to squeeze out between the end of the new wood fence and the wire property fence. Pretty sneaky! We put a temporary barrier there until Bert could put something more permanent in. Chief was obviously not impressed by being left. Which he proved again the next morning, when he squeezed out the other end of the yard the exact same way. Chief Houdini had struck again! Bert was finally able to put a post in at the end of both fences so the escape route was now impassable. To show us his unhappiness about this new situation Chief would drag, move, chew, and otherwise get into mischief all day. It was like a treasure hunt when I would get home. He loved to drag Jager's sheepskin bed out the dog door, carry our shoes and anything else that was left out everywhere (inside and out), take pieces from the inside log pile, chew them up and leave piles of wood everywhere, bring every toy he could find outside, he ate a small basket full of suet that my mom had hung for the birds (part of the basket was missing too), he had even gotten into the trash a few times. His days at home were apparently very busy. But how could I possibly be mad? He had been locked up for 5 years…he had done next to nothing wrong for having no idea how to be a dog. If this was going to be the worst, I could totally handle it. Besides, it gave me a reason to laugh every day when I got home.

My mom picks up the mail for us every day and leaves it on the washer, so I can check it out the minute I come through the door. Today there was a big manila envelope from the Beagle Freedom Project. I opened it up and found Chief's "dossier", with everything from his proof of rabies vaccination to his passport. My little laboratory beagle had a passport and it was even stamped inside! There was also a list and description of all the beagles that had come over. The descriptions said things like, very afraid of people (this one will need patient experienced dog owner), very friendly, scared of men, playful, had to have teeth pulled, or doesn't get along with other dogs, among other things. Some of the names didn't have descriptions next to them; I wasn't sure what that was an indication of. It was a definite reminder of everything Chief had been through and how far he had come in such a short amount of time. We had been given such an incredible opportunity here…I felt really lucky (and of course the tears started streaming).

Chief would show his dissatisfaction about staying home over the next few days by finding a new way to escape. There was no way he could squeeze out through the gate anywhere anymore, so he tried a new tactic. The longer and harder he would claw at the gate, the more the latch would bounce, the more the latch would bounce the easier it would be to push the gate open…Waa laa! Freedom. He did this a few times before we caught onto his scheme, new nick name Chief MacGyver. My mom had a great idea to tie a weight to piece of wire and hang it from the latch, a perfect, easy fix. No more escaping. He seemed to settle down after he realized we were coming back after awhile and he was still going to be able to go. He had caught the "five acres is simply not enough" disease from the other guys; he had come down with that pretty quickly.

Chapter 40

Home Visit

Today was the day Jean was coming for our home visit. I was nervous, excited, proud and a multitude of other emotions. Bert had taken the dogs to work for a short day so they could all have a good run and was home, luckily, before Jean arrived. Meanwhile, I left work as soon as the bell rung to clean up the house and prepare some snacks for Jean.

Bert was laughing at me…"She's not here to make sure our house is spotless!" he said, "She's coming to make sure he is happy, healthy and safe!" I knew he was right but I wanted to make such a good impression, I wanted our forever home to be the best (I'm not competitive…at all). We went about our afternoon chores when Jean pulled up to the gate. She was greeted by three baying beagles and a barking bird dog. We held onto all the puppies and opened the gate to let her in. When she drove in I noticed she had two dogs of her own in the car. Visitors!

Jean left the dogs in the car but I assured her they were more than welcome to get out after such a long drive. She looked around and said (to my complete and utter joy), "This is amazing! He definitely scored!" She let her dogs out and after the butt sniffing and jumping around, they all took off together. We all just stood watching and chatting for awhile, talking about the incredible strides he had made and what he had been doing. Jean said," One of the greatest things about this part of the job is showing up to an adopter's house and not even recognizing the dog they rescued!" I was beaming!

We walked down to see the horses when all of a sudden; her puppy caught sight of them and had a "puppy melt down". He stopped in his tracks and barked and barked and whined and wouldn't move. I haven't really dealt with dogs that haven't ever seen a horse before, well there was Chief not so long ago…but his reaction was nowhere near normal. Jean walked over, picked him up and carried him a bit closer to the huge animals, he seemed a little more confident in her arms, and just watched them intently. Meanwhile, Chief was taking her other dog for the short version of the property tour. Unfortunately, Jean had to do another home visit some distance away and wasn't going to be able to stay long. We went inside, dogs too, and her first words when she came in were, "This looks like a happy house where happy dogs live!" She was, of course, referring to ALL the dog toys spread all over the place, the bags of dog treats on the counter, the numerous dog beds, and on our "family" picture wall…a multitude of photographs of all the dogs. She stayed for a bit longer then loaded up her dogs and headed off to the next home. My feeling of complete satisfaction was unbelievable. Not that I thought Jean would show up and be unhappy with Chief's situation, or that she would take him away from us, but I felt like a weight had been lifted now that this visit was over. He was ours fair and square!

Chapter 41

Weather

Chief made me realize how much one takes weather for granted. But…when you've lived in a cage, inside, at a fixed temperature for your entire life, changes in the weather can be pretty exciting. In the little over two months Chief had been with us we had just about every type of weather one could experience. When he first came to us we were going through a heat spell. He did not like the heat, we figured he was used to being at a cool sixty five degrees or so 24/7 in the lab. Not long after that we finally got some much needed rain. We had forgotten that he had never been rained on until we watched him running around trying to dodge the drops. He finally sat under cover staring at the drops hitting the ground, then looking up to see if he could figure out where they were coming from. He didn't seem to mind being out in it after awhile and definitely loved the mud. This was one of those many times I wished he could speak to me in that Antonio Banderas voice of his and tell me exactly what he was thinking.

I thought we were at the end of our weather when we were lucky enough to get an early spring snow. Quite a bit of snow at that. All of our dogs love the snow and once they get past the fact that it goes up to their bellies and freezes their "unmentionables" it's all out. Chief, on the other hand, hadn't figured that out yet.

Chief's first snow on the ranch

Chief played in it all day, ending up with a coat of ice

He went flying out the dog door and if it had been possible for him to stop in midair and turnaround he would have. He landed in the drift that had built up over night outside our door and froze (literally and figuratively). It just so happened that right at that moment, all the other dogs came flying out of the dog door too. They, however, knowing the drill, took off like bullets into the snow. Not wanting to be left behind Chief did his best to maneuver through the snow after them. The best way to describe his gait was a cross between a long legged spider and a new born deer. It was hilarious to watch him try to get through the snow without it touching his belly or "unmentionables". He kept looking back at me as if to say, "Really?"

However, when the others disappeared around the corner of the house...he decided to suck it up and go with them. From then on he was like a sled dog in a beagle's body. We decided that his huge spread out paws were like snow shoes that helped him stay on top of the snow. Perhaps, if it is possible to have bonuses from laboratory life built in snow shoes might be one. He ran everywhere...ears flopping, tongue hanging out, tail wagging like a flag. He loved it. Watching them all tear around in the fresh snow with each other was great. It was almost like they were playing tag. Some spots in the snow were deeper than others so as they were running they would, all of a sudden, disappear. A few seconds later they would reappear covered in snow with a very shocked expression on their faces. Exhausted and near frozen we all went back into the house to warm up by the fire.

Weather...you've got to love it!

Chapter 42

No News

The busy horse show season was starting to pick up for Bert and he was off to another job site. I was a little worried (surprise, surprise) about this one. This particular piece of property is very large and there is a lot more terrain than where Chief had already been. It would be a lot harder to keep track of him and the other beagles pretty much say "bye" to Bert in the morning and don't come back until it's time to leave in the evening, so they would offer no guidance. I was just so glad that Bert was willing to take this part of Chief's "training" on so I could just hear the stories when he got home. The other problem with this site is there is NO cell service, so I couldn't get my updates throughout the day. Bert was probably okay with this so I wouldn't be bugging him all day, I on the other hand, would be a nervous wreck until they all pulled into the driveway.

They all piled into the truck that first morning and I kissed them all on the nose…I kissed Bert on the lips…and begged him to keep a good eye on Chief. He assured me he would, rolled up the window, and they were off. Then, nothing, all day, it killed me not to know what was going on! It was about five o'clock when they rolled in and I, of course, ran out to the truck for the official head count. Whew! All puppies were present and accounted for, now I could hear about the day.

To my surprise, there wasn't much of a story. Bert told me that Chief was a superstar; he had stuck around all day, never ventured far from where Bert was working, even though the other two had taken off for the entire day. That was it? He was a superstar, no drama, no disappearing, no chasing, no…nothing? I was in shock, I was so happy, I was speechless. "Are you serious?" was all I could manage. Bert answered; "Yep!" hopped out of the truck like it was no big deal and went inside. But, when we all got inside, we made a huge deal out of him.

The next morning, we went through the same routine. I waited patiently all day for my "boring" report of the day. However, today when they all piled out of the truck, there was a little more to the story, than the day before. "Today, Chief got lost for a little while," Bert began, with a smirk on his face. "Today…Chief found something big, dead, and smelly. He decided to take some "to go", after he rolled in it and was sufficiently smelly, found a nice bush to sit under, and didn't follow us when we left." I think right as Bert got to the "rolling in it" part I already had my arms wrapped around Chief and my nose almost buried in his face, when I smelled "it". Whatever "it" was, Bert was right…he had done a very sufficient job of getting smelly. New nickname Chief Stinky Face.

Luckily, Bert hadn't gotten too far away before he realized he had "misplaced" something and was able to retrace his steps to find Chief Stinky Face eating something dead and disgusting under a bush. The rest of the day went without incident. He was a half superstar today but was becoming more and more like a beagle every day. The first thing we did after story time was put Chief Stinky Face in the bathtub for a good scrub. The other guys were looking quite smug about not getting bathed too, but joined in the fun of running around the house with Chief when he was finished. We all climbed into bed after a long day, the beagles crashed in their spots and Bert and I reached all the way across three beagles for a kiss goodnight!

Chapter 43

The Canadian

House guests...some new people Chief hadn't met yet. One guest was a mild mannered, quiet man that would only be with us for a couple days, and only at night. He was the announcer (among other things) for the horse show that was about to begin. We help out with accommodations for people that come into town to work at the horse shows whenever we can, so Chief would have to get used to the occasional visitor. The other visitor would be with us for about two weeks and was anything but mild mannered and quiet; he was Bert's business partner and fellow course builder.

When Malcolm first got to the house, there was the usual "stranger danger" barking from the pack, which quickly died down when they saw the familiar face. Chief, on the other hand, hadn't had the pleasure of meeting Malcolm yet and wasn't one hundred percent convinced he wanted to be introduced. Malcolm already knew Chief's story, and being a dog person, understood how to approach the situation...treats. I've known Malcolm for a number of years, and honestly, never thought he would be sitting on the floor in the middle of my living room trying to coax my Spanish laboratory beagle to say "hi" with cookies. Chief is opening my eyes to new things every day. Chief was very timid, more so than I had seen him yet, which I thought surprising because Malcolm has such a calm air about him. He took a few cookies from him, but never really seemed comfortable around him. As the visit was a short and infrequent one, I wasn't too worried about it.

Then, there was Jay. Jay is a loud, large, block of a man. He has been building jumps with Bert for years and comes to stay with us twice a year for two to three weeks at a time. This visitor worried me for Chief's sake. He is a dog lover and has a pack of his own and I was hoping he would be sensitive to Chief's many idiosyncrasies. I was actually shocked by how well it went. We all decided that because Jay was with Chief and Bert all day outside, in the truck, and at home that Chief became used to having him around and wasn't bothered by the loud laugh or obnoxious behavior. I think it helped though, that Jay would keep treats in his pockets and give them to Chief whenever he would come around.

Chapter 44

A Lot to Love

Food motivation is a great tool…except when the subject starts to become as round as Chief was. Jay had no problem pointing out to us that Chief was FAT. I guess we already knew it but I have a tendency to rationalize my animal's weight issues away! I couldn't rationalize away the fact that after I had sent some new pictures of Chief to my sister she emailed a new nickname back to me…Chief Pudgy Bunny of the Ottoman Tribe. He was actually starting to look like a walking ottoman!

The very first time we had brought Chief to the vet was in January, he must have smelled it from a mile away. He wouldn't get out of the car and had to be dragged into the office and down the hall to the examination room. He weighed in at a solid forty pounds, got his microchip injected and we were on our way. Our vet mentioned that we may want to get a full blood panel done on him just to make sure everything was working the way it should because we had no idea what had been done to him. We would save that for the next visit…he wanted out!

Bert and I both agreed, during Jay's visit, that we had never seen a dog get so fat so fast. Chief was actually getting less food than the others and we were now feeding him from one of those bowls that is designed to slow down fast eaters. He got a very small snack in the morning and the treats he did get were only small pieces. He was still eating copious amounts of horse manure and since his discovery of yummy dead things...who knows what he was snacking on throughout the day. He was also spending all day out and about with Bert at work. As compared to living in a cage, his amount of exercise had increased over one hundred percent. The joke became that he was being used for diet pill testing while at the lab and now that he was off the diet, he was rebounding. I started to worry (again) that maybe something was out of whack with his system, so I called to make an appointment for the blood panel and also to check his thyroid levels.

Again, poor Chief wanted nothing to do with our wonderful vet! I had to drag him inside and up on to the scale...51 pounds. WHAT? He had gained eleven pounds in two months? That's impossible...not really, I was looking right at the scale and it said 50.8 pounds. That's it, there had to be something amiss with his system. The girls struggled to pick him up and carry him away to take his blood and clip his claws. When they brought him back, we went into an examination room and waited for Doc. Chief was glued to me and crawled into my lap with his nose in my armpit (all 50.8 pounds of him) while we waited. He jumped when the door opened and Doc came in for our chat. He asked me what was going on and how the patient was doing. All I could say was, "Doc, he's fat!" I explained all the "precautions" we were taking so he only ate his food, that we had cut back on treats, how much exercise he was getting etc. He said he would take a look at all the blood work and get back to me as soon as he knew anything. As soon as I stood up, Chief bolted for the door, and we were out of there.

I didn't want anything to be wrong with Chief, but I was hoping for an answer, other than "feed him less", for the weight gain. Doc called a few days later with great news…"It's your fault," he said. "Feed him less, everything looks fine!"

Whew! Feed him less…he acted like he was starving, although he very obviously was not, maybe just a little less. I would break us all into "a little less" slowly; at least the Pudgy Bunny was healthy.

Chapter 45

Spring Break

With the horse show season came many, many trips out of town for Bert, trips he would not be able to take the dogs on. Luckily, for me and the dogs, one of these trips was over my Spring break, a much needed week off for me and a week of not being left alone for the puppies. I don't consider myself a timid or scared individual, but when it came to Chief and letting him experience his independence...I was petrified. I was so worried about him getting lost and not being able to find his way home, even though he was doing a great job being free and on his own with Bert. Well, I considered this week to be a perfect opportunity for me to get over these feelings so the dogs could start going on trail rides with me again.

The first day of vacation, I woke up early to feed (all the dogs came out to help of course) and then we all jumped back into bed for a cuddle and a late sleep. I was so happy that they all actually wanted to cuddle and sleep in too. After some coffee and breakfast I decided we would venture out onto the property across from our house with no leash. I was feeling brave and confident. Armed with a bag of jerky treats, my plan was to use small pieces (because we were doing "a little less") of jerky as treats whenever he would come to me. I opened the gate and they were off. Chief took off with all of them and I found myself already stressing out about losing sight of him. Calm down. I just kept walking across the road and started down the trail that I take the horses on. I finally caught sight of Chief trotting around in the bushes, but going the opposite way. I kept walking slowly and called him a few times; he looked at me, turned around and trotted down the road toward me. Woo hoo! Success! Jerky! I gave him a little piece and just kept on walking. He wandered off the trail and rummaged around through the bushes always at that purposeful trot. When he would come back to me to check in, he would get that little treat.

He stayed on his own most of the time but followed me around the entire loop that I do with the horses. He disappeared momentarily only a few times but always came back to let me know he was around. By the time we were walking towards home I could tell he was exhausted. The tongue was almost dragging on the ground, the pace had gone from that purposeful trot, to an aimless, dragging walk that was so slow I was having a hard time keeping back with him. I was so proud of myself for not stressing and trusting him enough to just let go. I was so proud of him for proving to me that my fear was completely unfounded. We walked through the gate, closed it behind us and laid down in the grass to wait for the other two that were still out rampaging. It only took him a second to roll over on his side and fall asleep.

The next day, both of us feeling very cocky, went out again. He took off with the other guys again, only this time I wasn't stressing but feeling excited about what we would accomplish this outing. Today, Chief was very much in tune with the other two beagles. At one point they both started to sound off and took off down the trail, Chief took off with them. I just kept walking but went towards where they had gone to see what was going on. It was hysterical to watch. I enjoy watching Cowboy and Indian when they get on a scent because their tails have a different wag and they make this "chuffling "noise while they are sniffing the ground. They act like there is a string attached to their noses and it is just pulling them in all different directions. When I got to the three of them Cowboy and Indian were doing the usual, Chief on the other hand, wasn't really sure what to do. He just kind of followed them around not really sniffing the ground or looking for anything, just trying to be in it. It was great…he was trying to figure out what they were doing and why. He eventually lost interest and we were off again in another direction.

It was a successful walk. He followed me again all the way around the loop and I even added on another part. Chief would come back and visit for a little piece of jerky, then toodle off again. I was so proud of him. We were almost home and he was looking exhausted when, from the distance, we heard Cowboy and Indian sound off. We both stopped, turned around toward the sound, and Chief took off! For his size, he was running really fast. There I was, standing in the middle of the trail just watching him take off to who knows where (I don't even think he really knew where) debating. Do I try to catch up and follow? Do I chill out, wait and hope for the best? Do I start calling him waving my jerky bag in the air? Do I stand here frozen asking myself all these ridiculous questions? Finally, I decided…I'm just going to casually wait here, maybe meander down the trail a little way, but give him about twenty minutes before I completely freak out and panic.

It was hard, I mean really hard, to just stand there and wait. Just as I was about to lose it, I caught sight of him making his way back through the sage brush. I couldn't believe it. I started calling him in a super high pitched, squeaky voice over and over, the more I did it, the faster he ran toward me It was awesome. I luckily had a fairly good sized piece of jerky left and gave him half of it when he finally reached me. I saved the rest of it for when we were actually inside the gate. We crashed out on the grass like the day before to wait for the other guys.

We went out two or three more times during my vacation but I never quite got to the comfort level of going out on horseback. We would have to wait until Bert came home to try that one. I was so happy with his progress on our walks that I didn't want to ruin my confidence by losing him while I was riding. All these great days of exercise were tuckering everyone out and they didn't seem to mind staying home with me. It was going to be hard to head back to work after so many remarkable days. But the end of vacation was quickly approaching and Bert wouldn't be home for another week so the puppies would have to get used to being alone again.

Chapter 46

Is It Alive...

Back to work. The puppies fell right back into the routine, sad faces and all. Chief was actually very well behaved, I didn't find anything out of place, eaten, outside, or disturbed. I was very impressed. However, after a few days of being left alone I did find something that I was not very impressed by. I came home to the pile of puppy love on the rug in the hall way that always made me feel better. From there we went to the bedroom where I changed into my "uniform" for chores and got down on the floor to snuggle with Indian who was laying on his back just waiting for a good rub. As I was kissing his face, rubbing his tummy, and burying my face in his fur, I just happened to take a sideways glance and see two toys (or skins as we call them)sitting side by side not far from Indian's head. After my double take, I realized that one of them was not a toy at all, in fact the huge yellow front teeth, and the scaly little tail made it incredibly clear that this was a real gopher!

After the initial shock wore off, I proceeded to the bathroom to rinse off my face and rinse out my mouth. I had to take a picture of the two "toys" sitting next to each other with my phone and send it to Bert with the caption, "Is it live? Or is it Memorex?" When I returned, Shminny was sitting next to his little friend, guarding it from the others. I knew

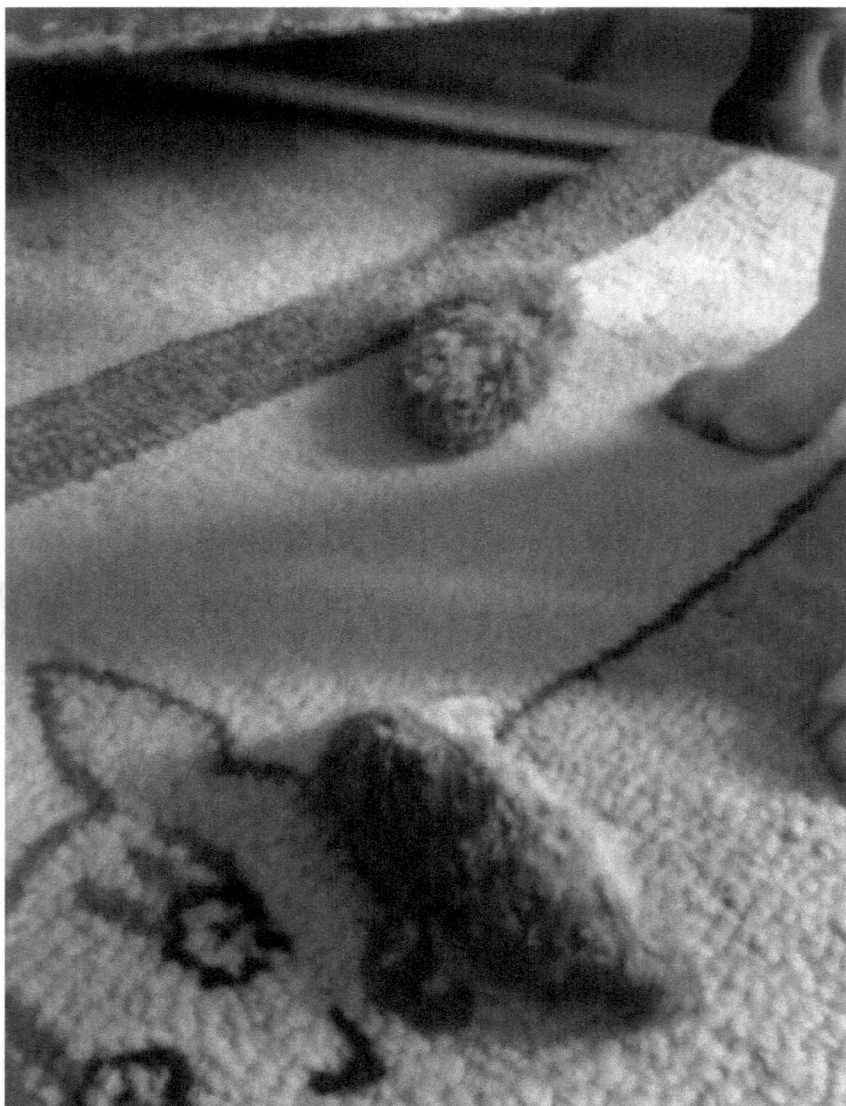

Is it alive…or is it Memorex?

I looked over to see long yellow teeth…

if I tried to get it away from him he wouldn't let me so I decided to go outside with everyone and try to get him to follow us out. Don't get me wrong…we have a gopher epidemic so any help the dogs can give us on that front is greatly appreciated. I would just prefer not to find them in the house.

We all made it outside and Shmin was having a hard time deciding if he wanted to play, or carry a dead thing around in his mouth. He also had a shadow; Chief was stalking him to see what would transpire with the little goodie that he was carrying. Indian is the only dog out of the three that doesn't eat what he catches; both Cows and Jager will usually eat what they catch. We weren't sure what Chief would do yet, as he hadn't caught anything but if this followed the way he was with all other consumable items…he would eat whatever he caught. Indian finally decided playing was a better idea. He left his little prize in the grass and took off for bigger and better things. Chief took the opportunity to grab the gopher and in a few quick gulps…it was gone. Well, he answered that question. They all found something to do that involved their complete attention and before I knew it…they had caught another gopher that Chief somehow ended up with. I only caught sight of the tail end of it before it went down the hatch! Two gophers in one day…he wouldn't want dinner would he? Yeah right.

Chapter 47

Trail Ride

Bert arrived home and we were able to take the pooches for a few good runs down at the show grounds. I was ready...ready for a trail ride. I thought with Bert home, I could take the dogs out with me and if I lost track of Chief, I could call Bert and tell him where I had lost him. Then he could walk out on the trails and try to find him. Easy, shmeezy, I wouldn't have to worry at all!

I decided to take Mama for Chief's first excursion into the wilds. She is a very patient horse and wouldn't mind stopping frequently to wait if we needed to. We were ready to go and the other guys all ran down to the gate to be let out, Chief followed them but kept looking back at me to make sure it was okay that he was out and actually coming along. He didn't seem phased by Mama walking behind him and as soon as I opened the gate, he took off. He followed the path we had taken together, and occasionally went off into the bushes, but always came back to check in. I was feeling so confident.

We had only been out a few minutes when Cowboy and Indian found a scent and went bonkers! They bolted, sounding off the entire way. I was watching to see what Chief would do, and sure enough, he took off right after them. Still feeling quite confident, I didn't worry where he had gone, I just kept Mama on our usual trail. When I reached the point of impatience (it had been about ten minutes) I started to call his name, but I kept walking. I got to the top of a hill that gave me a great view of the surrounding area. I stopped here to look around and keep calling. After about five minutes…Chief came out of the bushes and walked right up to Mama, close enough that I could throw him a piece of jerky that he would be able to find. Wow! This was going remarkably well. So well, I thought I would tempt fate and keep going. I turned Mama around and we continued on down the trail, all the boys joined us and we must have looked like the local valley hunt club, horses and hounds.

My luck was about to turn…we got into another area of thick underbrush and all three beagles disappeared together, which at the time, I thought was good. I kept going and heard the occasional howl from one of the beagles which told me in which general direction they were. Then, it went silent…nothing. Okay, I admit it, I panicked! I hadn't seen him for awhile and I hadn't heard anything for awhile. I started to call and call while I was heading home hoping he would start to follow me in that direction. I couldn't handle it any longer! I was calling in the reinforcements. I called Bert and told him that I had lost him and about where it was I had last seen him. I started to get mad at myself, I should've headed back when I found him the first time, I shouldn't have let him disappear for so long…shoulda, coulda, woulda.

I headed back home, still calling when I met up with Bert walking down the road toward where I had last seen him. I asked him what I should do, he told me to go home and wait, he was sure Chief would meet me there soon. He told me that Chief had been "lost" before and never stayed away for too long. I wasn't on the verge of tears yet, but if he didn't come back soon, I would be. I got back home, cleaned up Mama and put her away. Jager had come home awhile ago and was enjoying the sunshine on the grass with no idea of my mounting fear for his new brother.

I heard Cowboy and Indian sounding off way off in the distance and knew they wouldn't be back for awhile. We luckily had about two more hours of daylight left, so I had two more hours to NOT worry about coyotes on top of everything else I was worrying about. It had been about thirty minutes since I had last seen him, I called Bert to get an update and he told me he hadn't seen him and that he hadn't heard anything from the other two. I asked him again what I should do. He told me to get in the truck and drive down the road, maybe the sound of the truck would be familiar enough to lure him out of the bushes. Right as I was about to get in the truck, I heard my mom calling from the gate. When I headed in that direction, I saw Cows and Shmin running in the gate. Unfortunately, just two, although very glad they were back safe, I was just hoping to see all three of them.

I got into the truck and had just started going down the road, when I saw Bert walking in on the trail. No puppy. Okay, I started to cry. Now I was really mad at myself. Bert joined me in the truck and assured me it would be alright and tried to make me laugh by telling me that Chief would be on his way home because it was dinner time, and there is no way he would miss that! He did make me chuckle a little bit. We were almost to the end of the road. I had my head out the window the whole way calling for him. We had gotten to a point in the road where the horse path that we take crosses it and goes down into an overgrown area. This is also where the path starts to head for home. About twenty yards in front of us, Chief was trotting across the road and just about to head down the path. I called his name and he looked right at us but seemed unsure of the truck. I jumped out and called again. This time he recognized me and ran to me with his tail up and wagging! I picked up all fifty one pounds of him and squeezed him as hard as I could. I just kept saying, over and over again, "You scared me Beefy!" While crying of course. We climbed into the truck and he crawled over to Bert's lap. Bert gave him a squeeze and just said, "Beefers, you scared mama!" I think, although he wouldn't admit it, he had been a bit worried too.

He was obviously exhausted. His tongue was as far out as it could go, he was panting deeply and quickly, and he acted like his legs were made out of rubber. When we finally got home, we found out that Indian had dug out under the gate as soon as I pulled out with my truck. I felt like screaming. Bert gave one of those loud ear piercing whistles and, to my surprise; Shmin came flying down the road and right in the gate. Whew! Every puppy was present and accounted for. Who knew something as enjoyable and relaxing as a trail ride would turn into such a fiasco.

The first thing I said to Bert after things calmed down was, "I knew we weren't ready for that yet!" Yet again, he brought up some very valid points..."He was on his way home, you said yourself that is where the trail starts to head for home. He wasn't really gone that long! He was probably following the sounds from the other two but by the time he got there they had already moved on so he just kept on following them. I think it was actually a pretty good first go!"

Okay, okay! So he made some great points, Chief was following the trail that we had walked together. He was heading home, and he hadn't really been gone long enough to be classified as "missing". All I knew was that it was scary, that feeling of guilt I had was amazing. I couldn't believe that I had lost him. We would definitely do it again, but only with "backup" and only when there would be ample daylight to look for him if need be. Needless to say they all slept like rocks and Chief got extra hugs and snuggles.

Chapter 48

Too Hot!

Another hot spell. We were quickly discovering that Chief was not a fan of the heat. In fact, he hated it. Because Bert was out of town, there was no way I was going to try the whole trail riding thing again so I was on foot. I wanted to let them out for a good run because they had been cooped up all week, so I tried to get a fairly early start before it got too hot. Well I wasn't quite early enough. I opened the gate and all the dogs took off across the street into the field. Cows and Indian got on a scent right away and disappeared in an instant, Chief wasn't far behind. I just walked slowly down the trail with Jager behind me.

After ten minutes or so, Chief came back for his jerky fly by and then was off again for some exploring. We were about half way around the loop and the temperature was rising quickly I started to notice that Chief's purposeful trot was turning into a dragging walk. I also started noticing that he was trying his hardest to walk in the shadows of all the bushes instead of the full sun on the trail. Finally, at one point he stopped moving all together and just threw himself down in the cool grass under a small oak tree. That was it! He was breathing so hard, his tongue was hanging out in the grass, and his eyes were rolled back in his head. I took a couple quick pictures with my phone and sent a message to Bert that just said, "It's too hot!" I have to admit, I remembered that

It's too hot!

To my surprise, he was passed out under a tree!

he had come to us with a "slight heart murmur" so watching him lying there under the tree breathing so hard worried me.

I gave him a few minutes to regain his strength before we headed back to the house. The heat didn't seem to bother the other two... I heard them sounding off on a scent somewhere far away. So, it was Jager who was not looking so hot, or I guess I should say he was looking incredibly overheated, Chief who was walking so slowly I had to keep stopping for him to catch up and me on the long walk home. When we finally made it home, Chief crashed in my mom's grass that was wet and cool and Jager went to drink all of the water out of her watering can. Not long after we returned, the other beagles joined us on the wet grass to cool off and calm down. Note to self...no long walks in the heat for the Chief.

Chapter 49

The Skip Loader

Today was perhaps one of the most incredible days for the Beefers. Bert came back from a short out of town trip and was taking all the dogs to work...they were all very excited about this. It hadn't cooled down much so I wasn't expecting too much of a story from Bert. I was wrong.

Bert had gotten home before I did and none of the dogs came out to greet me...they must have had a great run and couldn't possibly get off the couch for me! I walked quietly in the house and saw Bert comfortably reclining in his chair watching ESPN; Jager curled up in his chair, and the beagle train on the couch. Home sweet home. As soon as Bert looked at me...I got dog piled. Everybody got up to greet me, and Bert said, "Mr. Chief had a HUGE day today." As I was being kissed and jumped on by Chief I was dying to know what had happened.

Bert has been telling me all along, since day one with him at work, how frightened Chief was of the skip loader. This is a huge, loud, yellow piece of equipment that he uses just about every day to move jumps, dirt, rocks, and any number of other things. I knew that Chief steered clear whenever Bert was on it because he was petrified of everything about it. So when Bert started the story by telling me that Chief was trotting alongside the skip loader as he was moving a jump, I was already amazed. I thought that was the story. I was about to be really impressed until the story kept going. He continued on to tell me that when he finished unhooking the jump he lifted Chief up onto the skip loader for a ride. Bert said he stayed perfectly still for the first part of the ride then, he got a little spooked and tried to get behind the seat. Being the size that he is now, he actually got stuck! Bert had to reach in from behind the seat and lift him out because he couldn't get him out any other way. Chief started squealing because he really doesn't like to be picked up, but as soon as Bert put him down everything was fine. So fine, in fact, he let Bert put him back in the skip loader (on the seat this time) for another ride. This went much better; he apparently likes the driver's seat. New nick name Captain Chief.

This was yet another one of those times Bert and I stopped and thought about this amazing dog. How many hurdles he had gotten over, how many hoops he had jumped through, how far he had come from a cage to riding in the captain's seat of a skip loader. It was absolutely staggering. We had been witnesses to it all, we were so lucky to be a part of this and of his life. Okay, enough...I didn't want to start crying again. He seemed to have that effect on me, in a good way of course.

Chapter 50

A Second Try

The count down to the summer trip to Montana was on. Bert would be leaving the first of June for a quick stop at a site in Washington then on to Montana. I wouldn't be joining him until the end of June. We still hadn't decided who was taking which dogs. Of course, I wanted Bert to take all four dogs because I was bringing the two horses and was already having a nervous breakdown about making the trip on my own. Bert on the other hand only wanted to bring two of them because finding a hotel with four dogs was going to be a nightmare. Needless to say we would be going back and forth on this subject for a while.

Meanwhile, Chief continued to make great strides every day. Bert was out of town again for another show in Northern California. The dogs were no longer allowed to attend this particular venue due to the fact that Indian had been hit by a car chasing one of the MANY coyotes that frequented the property. The dogs were also always getting into trouble with the boarders and visitors as this venue was also a public boarding facility and dog park. So they were stuck at home with me… again.

I knew the first morning I woke up, after Bert left, surrounded by beagles that today was a perfect day to try another trail ride for the Beefers. We would get an early start so if things should go awry I would have enough time to search for him. Most importantly we would get out before it was too hot.

I decided to take Mama out because not only is she very level headed, but if I was to start having a panic attack, she would not let my nervousness affect her. Cowboy, Indian, and Jager have all become exceptionally good at knowing when we are going out for a trail ride. They all get very excited, start jumping around, and run right for the gate. Chief was beginning to get the hang of the whole ritual; however he still hadn't mastered the getting excited and jumping around part. He fell right into his purposeful trot and headed for the gate with the pack. We were on our way.

It was already ridiculously hot but I thought that might work to my advantage. Chiefer Beefer moves much slower in the heat, I might be able to keep closer tabs on him! Well, my plan didn't necessarily work, he was off and trotting, He stayed nearby as we headed down the trail, meandering in and out of the bushes. He still wasn't a huge fan of "off roading" and stuck mostly to the horse trails. Cows and Shmin were off as usual and I all I could see was the white tips of their tails, like flags, disappearing into the brush. Jager, in his old age, was becoming less adventurous and stayed on the trail behind me and sometimes just headed home when he was ready.

I continued down the trail and was very impressed with how calm and relaxed I was keeping myself. I arrived at my lookout spot, waited a few moments, and... there he was! No calling, no panicking ...just Chief in all his huffing and puffing glory. I made a huge, high pitched, deal out of him and tossed him a small piece of jerky. I have to admit, I was fairly worried about continuing on. This is where I had "lost" him before, but the only way we were going to get better at this whole thing was to keep trying, so I gave Mama a nudge and we were off again.

As I kept going along the trail, I kept talking to Mama, the birds, myself…anything to make some kind of sounds that Chief would be able to hear and hopefully follow. I periodically turned around to look back down the trail, so far so good. There he was, tongue hanging out, trotting right down the trail. I lost him for a bit when the brush became thick but was always able to catch a glimpse of him following the trail. And so we continued the entire way home.

Holy Cow! We did it. We got to the gate almost as we had left it! Mama, Cows, Shmin, and Chief Trail Boss. I closed up the gate behind us and hopped off Mama. I was surrounded by hot, panting puppies and praised all of them with pats, squeals, and kisses. I felt huge! I stayed calm the entire time, and Chief had done it all on his own. I didn't want to get too cocky…one trail ride did not a trail dog make; we still had quite a bit of work to do. But I couldn't help but be crazy proud of him.

When Bert called that night I spent the entire phone call gushing about how well Chief had done that day. He was just as excited as I was and said, "I knew he would get it! He's so smart!" This was one of those instances I was happy to admit that Bert is usually right.

Chapter 51

Trail Boss

Sunday morning! We were going to give it another try, hopefully with the same results. Chief Trail Boss headed out the gate with the rest of us like he had been doing it for years. I followed the same trail we had used the day before and he was right there the entire time. We got a later start than we had the day before so it was quite bit hotter by the time we hit the trail. I noticed Chief Droopy Drawers was back! He stayed in the shadows when he could and if he caught up with me he would take a second to sit down under a bush. But, no matter how far behind he got, he would stay on the trail and just keep plugging along. Once again, we got back to the gate just as we had left it. I think we had it. Two great days in a row. Chief was on his way to becoming a full-fledged beagle.

I decided week days wouldn't be good days to take the new trail boss out, I was getting home from work too late to allow enough time for any problems. We had two more weekends of perfect trail rides, Chief was even starting to wander off the trail and do a little four wheel driving. I noticed something about him on our fourth or fifth outing that baffled my mind. Chief could always be found following the trail or very close to it, I followed a loop where at some points you could see parts of the trail where you had already been or were going to. A few times I would spot Chief on another part of the trail and call to him to try and get him to cut across and join me. He would stop look right at me, look down the trail, look at me again, then turn and head down the trail at his purposeful trot. Well, I had taught him well, he would not leave the trail, even if I wanted him to. Chief Must Follow the Trail was very predictable and usually easy to find if he fell behind! I no longer had to worry that he would get lost or run off. I think that up to this point, even though he had had so many breakthroughs, this may have been one of the biggest ones. From a cage to being completely free; out in the open spaces, coming back all on his own, knowing his way around out in the middle of nowhere...it was unbelievable. But watching it all happen in front of my eyes made it believable.

Chapter 52

The Babysitter

Well, if the trail ride breakthrough was not enough, Chief's next assignment was going to be a big one. I was going to be joining Bert in Northern California to compete at an event with my two horses, but no dogs! So, Mom was going to be in charge of three lonely beagles, Bert was taking Jager with him on most trips because he was getting worried about how much longer he was going to be around. It would be Chief's first extended alone time. The other guys didn't like to be left alone for days but they were used to it, Chief, on the other hand, and never been left alone for more than a day.

The boys have a knack for knowing when either one of us is leaving for more than a day. When Jager sees Bert's duffle bag he will usually go outside and park himself right under Bert's truck. Cows and Indy will usually attach themselves to whomever is leaving and make it impossible to get ready to do so. Chief was not privy to these rituals and was happy enough following me around as I loaded up the horse trailer, went in and out of the house, and packed my bags. I was going to be leaving at three o'clock in the morning and was hoping it would be easy to slip out while everyone was too sleepy to realize what was going on...no such luck! All three dogs were up and out before I was even dressed. So I decided to let them stay out with me while I loaded my bags into my truck and the horses on to the trailer. However, then trying to get them wrangled into the house was an experiment. Luckily, my mom had gotten up to help out and say good bye…she stood at one end of the fence, I stood at the other and we eventually met at the dog door and funneled them straight in. Success.

I was off. I promised to call my mom often to check on the guys and told her to call the vet for anything. This was going to be hard. I had been on the road for only a few hours and already missed them! When I pulled on to the show grounds, first I called Bert to let him know I had arrived, second, I called my mom to let her know I had arrived and to ask how things were going. She told me that after I had left, all the boys had gone back in, gotten on the bed and gone back to sleep until she went out to feed Mo and open the door so they could use the doggie door. For the next two days, Chief stayed outside with mom while she worked out in the yard, sat with her on the couch while she was there watching TV in the evenings and slept on the bed with Cows and Indy at night.

On Friday evening, my sister came up to spend the weekend in the "country" with mom. The boys were all very pleased to have her as she slept in the guest room at our house so there was a warm body there for them. I did, however, forget to warn my sister about Chief the Thief and leaving things on the floor! When I called for my update he had apparently earned himself a new nickname…the Bragle. Not thinking that anything would leave the guest room floor, Gwen had left the door open while she was out and about. Little did she know that Chief the Thief had struck and removed something from her room. The next morning while trying to get dressed to go...Gwen realized something was missing. At that moment in walked mom with a dusty but intact, lacey, colorful bra. And with that, the Bragle was crowned I returned home that night very late but was met by three very excited beagles and we spent awhile rolling around on the floor laughing, kissing, licking, and there may have even been squealing. Chief had passed another test with flying colors. Five days without Bert or I, just mom and he had done wonderfully; in fact, he and mom had become quite close.

Chapter 53

The Diet

Well, it had come time for the final decision to be made about who Bert would be taking with him to Montana. I gave up trying to get him to take all four of the boys and settled with his decision to take Jager and Chief. His reasoning made sense... Cows and Shmin were seasoned travelers so they would be very low stress for me to handle while hauling the two horses. Jager and Chief had become buddies, the best one could become with a grouch like Jager, and Jager was also a seasoned traveler so Bert would be able to focus on Chief. None of his confidence, however, would stop me from worrying everyday about what Chief was doing, not doing, eating, drinking, rolling in, being scared of, not being scared of...I would be a mess.

In the five, almost six, months Chief had been with us he had put on weight...a lot of weight. He was filling up daily on horse manure and had discovered that what the horses ate was very yummy too. So while the horses were eating and dumping their food, supplements and all, out on to the ground, Chief Hoover was there to clean it up for them. All of this in addition to our need to make him as happy as possible was adding inches to his waistline. I decided to put him on "diet" food, which he didn't seem to mind as he was getting fed a cup in the morning and in the evening when the other guys would eat. Feeding time turned into a circus as I had to supervise to make sure Chief Hoover didn't get to anyone else's bowl that could possibly have a morsel of something in it. It still made me feel guilty to see him frantically finish his meal and run around to everyone else's acting as if he was still starving, when, very obviously, he was not. Chief had made it so far but I was beginning to think his food hang ups would be a permanent scar.

This new diet he was on was another source of concern when Bert decided to take him. I would have to send the food with him and hope it lasted until I got there because it was shipped to me every month; it was not something you could buy anywhere. I had to also trust that "dad" would not frequent fast food restaurants and decide that the dogs could just have that for dinner instead of his special food. I 'm not uptight about these dogs at all. I made Bert promise to keep Chief as strictly on his diet as possible…it didn't really help calm my mind though.

We packed up his truck with goodies for both dogs and humans. Bert packed his bag while I packed a bag for Chief and Jager. It was filled with leashes, harnesses, toys, treats (low fat), more toys, bowls, a few bottles of water and a towel. Jager had already caught on and was parked under Bert's truck ready to go. Chief, on the other hand, was completely clueless as to what was going on or that he was about to be in the truck for longer than he ever had been. Cows and Indy were pretty sure dad was leaving…again and were just waiting for their invitation to get in the truck. It was time for Bert to leave and he lifted Jager in the back seat and put Chief in the front seat, when he climbed in after a huge hug and a kiss from me, Cows and Indy realized their invitation was not coming. So as Bert backed out of the driveway, I cried…for many reasons. First, I was going to miss all of them, next I thought about all the adventures and firsts Chief was going to have that I was going to miss. I also knew that Bert's goal for Jager was to make it one more time to Montana; it was like Disneyland for him, I was afraid to think about what that meant. Then, of course, the selfish side of me would be lonely and dreading making this trip by myself. Cowboy, Indian, and I huddled in the driveway for a while, me crying, the dogs pouting and cuddling trying to make me feel better.

Chapter 54

The Trip

Finally…school was out! I couldn't have been happier.
I had never left so fast on the last day of school in all my years
of teaching. I would always hang around for a few hours
after school, go by the after-school program and say hi to any
of my students who were there…not his year. I had about
three weeks until I was to leave for Montana and could finally
be stress free, or so I though.

While I was happily preparing my two horses for our
biggest, toughest competition yet, I was in a constant state of
worry over what was happening with Chief while they were
on their adventure. Bert had phoned when they got to the
hotel that was mid-way between home and Washington. He
told me that Chief really didn't like the idea of the hotel, it
wasn't his "house" and every time there was a noise outside,
Jager would jump up and bark at the door. Poor Chief was
never able to relax, poor Bert wasn't able to get any sleep, and
good old Jager just kept on barking. Eventually, sometime
after midnight, he ended up putting them both in the truck
so he could get a few hours of sleep. When he was ready to
go, he walked out to the truck to see Chief and Jager curled
up in the back seat on the memory foam bed he had made for
them…snug as two bugs in a Ford. The night of no sleep was
forgiven and the adventure continued. After a total of twenty
hours, with stops of course, they reached the property in

Washington and an entire new world was open to Chief Explorer.

This particular property is a private residence as well as a practice facility so there is a house, a small barn, and lots of cats. Unfortunately, Jager has never been a fan of cats; he likes to chase them and has taught Cows and Indy to do the same. After Chief's innocent first meeting with my mom's cat, Bert and I were both interested to see what he would do with a cat outside. Well, we got our answer...nothing. He didn't pay a bit of attention to the, what seemed like hundreds, of cats walking around. What he did pay attention to was the numerous bowls of cat food placed throughout the barn and around the house. New nickname...Chief Meow Mix. There went the diet right out the door.

While working on the property Bert was staying with his new trainee, David, in a horse trailer that had very nice living quarters. The trailer was quite high off the ground and David's little Jack Russell, Muffin, was able to leap in and out with no problem. Jager with his nonexistent hip joints and Chief with his excess baggage weren't able to get in and out of the trailer with such ease. So Bert and David spent more than a little time building some steps for the two dogs to use, which they didn't and ended up being lifted in and out of the door for the duration. The first night, after an exhausting first day on the "farm" Bert got to cuddle with Chief and Muffin while Jager slept in a comfy bed on the floor.

Second day on the job meant actually trying to get something accomplished. Bert climbed up into the tractor and headed off to the far end of the property, when he turned around, there was Chief and Jager following right behind him. That fear of loud noises and huge machinery had definitely been conquered. After the "long run" following the tractor, Jager led Chief to the water jump for a cool off dip and a drink. Summer was already in full swing and it was hot! Chief loved the water and started heading over to the water on his own whenever he needed to cool down.

Perhaps the most exciting thing about this trip was finding out that Chief absolutely loved riding on the quad with Bert. In one of our nightly phone calls Bert told me the story of how he had climbed on the quad expecting Chief to follow him, when all of sudden Chief tried to jump up on the seat with him. Once Bert loaded him on, he became a permanent fixture whenever it was in use; in fact, even when Bert would get off, Chief would stay up on the seat hoping the ride wasn't really over. Chief Four Wheeler was born. I was overwhelmed to hear the story and even more overwhelmed when he emailed a picture of the two them. I was so proud of my boy. I forwarded the picture of Chief to Shannon at the Beagle Freedom Project to show her his progress. She was just as excited as I was.

I would like to say that all of Chief's new experiences were positive ones, however, some lessons he had to learn the hard way, especially when on a farm. Hot wire was one of those kinds of lessons. The property was surrounded by three rows of hot wire to keep things on the property and to keep things off the property. While Bert was working nearby Chief must have touched the wire with his paw, but all Bert heard was a horrible squeal and saw Chief hobbling towards

Let's go Dad!

Chief loved riding around the ranch on the quad

him on three legs. He stayed with Bert for hugs and reassurance for quite a while and spent the rest of the day limping on his front leg and staying very close to dad.

My nightly phone calls were so exciting and I looked forward to them every night. I wanted full details and insights, all of it. These were perhaps the longest most animated phone calls I had ever had with my husband in all our years of nightly phone calls! Bert has never been much of a talker but he had so much to tell me about these days with Chief, it was fantastic. I missed them so much and was feeling a bit left out that I couldn't be there to experience all these wonderful things with them. Meanwhile Chief and Jager were becoming closer and closer and Chief was becoming very patient with Jager's little outbursts, so much so Jager was realizing there was no point in barking and growling at him.

The work in Washington was finished so they all loaded into the truck to finish the trip to Montana. New state, new adventures, new people and I would be there soon.

Chapter 55

Updates

Cowboy, Indian, the horses and I were keeping ourselves busy getting ready for our big road trip. I luckily had talked a good friend of mine from work into accompanying me on the drive. Just knowing that had reduced my stress level by multitudes. Regina isn't a horse person but she is a level headed dog person and just the company was going to make the trip that much better. With that worry out of my way now all there was to think about was how Chief was doing with Bert.

They had gotten to the property in Montana which consists of about 600 acres of some of the most beautiful land I have ever seen. It is not only a beautiful piece of property but it is surrounded by the most spectacular country I have ever been in. The people that own this property put on the best and biggest horse show on the west coast and I am lucky enough to be able to work with Bert on the course as well as, this year, compete my two horses. The owners are very hospitable and don't mind the fact that our three, now four, dogs take over those 600 acres for the two months that we are there. Jager has been going for the entire eleven years the show has been running, Cows and Indian started going when they were just little puppies. They have all become part of the family. Chief was about to be initiated into that same Montana family.

In the two weeks Chief was there, my nightly updates were filled with stories of him becoming very independent, loving the water, following Jager everywhere, sticking around the "shop" with the guys , following the tractor around, riding in the Mule, playing with Muffin, passing out every night with dad, and having the best time ever! He had earned himself a new nickname…Chief Raccoon. Bert would tell me how Chief and Jager would disappear for extended periods of time and when they returned, Chief would always have some kind of food in his mouth. He would be able to find Cheetos buried in the truck under weeks of accumulated "stuff" or pick the mule that had the snacks in the glove box. Chief's nose was definitely working over time, but the fact that it was working, and that he was using it was so great. It was so hard not to come to tears almost every night hearing about this dog that had been experimented on, now running around on 600 acres completely on his own being the best dog he was learning how to be. I just couldn't wait to get there to see him in action.

In addition to the Chief updates, I had to make sure to check in on Jager. Before they left Jager had been having some pretty bad days as far as his old body was concerned. After all he was 19 years old. His entire hind end was giving out on him and all the pain killers in the world were no longer making any difference for him. It was hard to watch because he always wanted to "go", staying behind was not an option for him even if it meant dragging himself around. But then, he would be completely fine the next day, like he had never been sore. I wanted to make sure Bert was really keeping track of how he was doing and not denying the fact that there was a problem. I didn't really want to be "that person" that was negative all the time about his condition; I just wanted to make sure Bert was paying attention. He was.

Chapter 56

Snake Bite

At home we were going about our daily chores slowly packing and preparing for the trip. We live in an area where rattlesnakes are a constant danger. All the dogs have been getting the rattlesnake "vaccine" for the last couple years and Chief got his for the first time this year. I was never really clear what the vaccine actually did…well I was about to find out.

We were all out feeding the horses at about eight o'clock in the evening, because it was summer time it was still light out but starting to cool off. I had just thrown hay for Homes when Cowboy came flying across the pasture in a complete panic. When he got to me, he practically skidded into my leg whining and rubbing his muzzle with his paw. I immediately stopped what I was doing and looked him over; all I found was a small bloody spot just above his lip in his whiskers. I thought, at first, it may be a bee sting which worried me because Cows is very allergic to bees. However, the big fear in the back of my mind was a rattlesnake. It wasn't hard to talk myself out of it, after all, it was eight o'clock at night, it was on the property, there was only one hole…how could it be a snake bite? I called Bert, I called my horse vet, and I called the pet emergency hospital, which was over an hour away and finally decided he needed to go in. His face was swelling and his breathing was becoming rather raspy. My mom drove us and I wanted to bring Indian because I didn't want him to stay alone. He was very obviously worried about his brother as he kept sniffing his face and stayed in the back seat with him the entire way to the emergency hospital.

When we reached the hospital, Cows face was about 3 times the size it was supposed to be and he was in so much pain. I carried him into the waiting room where he was immediately taken from me and taken into the back. The ladies at the front desk told me they would do some blood tests to see if it was actually a rattlesnake bite and to what extent the venom had compromised his blood. I went out to sit with Indy and my mom while we waited. About a half hour later, the doctor came out and knocked on my mom's window. She told us that it was in fact a rattlesnake bite but he had been very lucky. It wasn't a full bite so the amount of venom was low, she felt it was probably a warning "snap" and because it was later in the evening and a bit cooler the snake wasn't at its full strength. However, Cows was going to have to spend the night to be monitored to make sure his blood was clotting the way it should be. They told me they would call if there were any changes but to plan on picking him up tomorrow afternoon. If this was the case, what in fact had the vaccine done for him, I wondered. I asked the vet that exact question, her answer was simple; "It bought him that hour or more that it took you to decide to bring him in and get here." Well, I couldn't argue with that! We drove home at about midnight, the entire time I squeezed Indy and wouldn't let him off my lap. He seemed to cuddle extra close that night.

In the two weeks Cows was recovering, Indy went to the vet at least three times to have foxtails pulled out of his nose and ears. It seemed every time we went out for a run, he came back with some foreign body lodged in some place it wasn't supposed to be. I had pretty much broken the bank with vet bills in the few weeks I was home...I think it was a sign that we were supposed to get going.

So we did.

Chapter 57

And We're Off

I was leaving two horses home for my mom to keep an eye on for us but that was it on the animal front. My friend, the dogs, the horses and I would be pulling out around midnight to miss the heat through the desert. I was nervous, excited, stressed, happy…all sorts of emotions that made it hard to sleep. Cows and Indy knew something was up and didn't really sleep either. Finally, we just decided to get started.

All the animals travelled like super stars. The horses hauled particularly well, and when we stopped for a few hours in Utah, they came out, ate, drank and rested like they had done this trip a thousand times before! Cows and Indy had actually done this trip, not a thousand, but many times and were handling it like pros. They ran around, chased things, dug holes, and napped. We ended up not staying the entire night and got started again around midnight which put us into Montana and pulling onto the property at about six in the morning.

I had called Bert to let him know we were pulling in so when we finally got out of the truck, all my boys were waiting for us. The puppies had an exceptionally happy reunion; I could only imagine Chief's Antonio Banderas voice talking a million miles an hour trying to tell about everything he had been doing since he left home. He even jumped up on my legs to say hi. I was so happy, for some reason I had worried that he might forget me…I was wrong. The hellos only took a few minutes and they were off, I mean gone, they literally disappeared on to "their" 600 acres. We unloaded the horses, tucked them into their huge, grassy pastures, unhooked the trailer and my friend and I headed into town to take a much needed nap. We made it…all in one piece and it felt so good to be there.

Chapter 58

Montana

The next three weeks consisted of a series of ten to twelve hour days which included preparing the horses for the upcoming competition, playing with the dogs, planning the decorations for the cross country course, playing with the dogs, going through all the flowers that would be used on the course, and more playing with the dogs. At this time in the summer it stays light until almost ten o'clock in the evening. It was hard to leave the property before eight and the dogs would be exhausted after a full day of running, hunting and swimming.

One morning on the way out to work one of the horses, we passed by a lake on the property where there is a fake coyote that is staked into the ground by the shore line. The coyote has been there for years and used to be covered with fake fur and would move due to a motion sensor inside of it. Jager leaves it alone but every year the Beagles go after it and act like it is a real animal. As Cows and Indy were having a fit of growling, barking and panicking about fifty feet from the coyote, Chief looked at them, looked at me, trotted right up to that coyote and sat down right next to it. I could just hear him saying, "Guys, guys it's not real, trust me, I've been here forever and it hasn't moved since I've been here." Finally every one settled down and remembered that this thing was in the same place every year. It was an extraordinary feeling to witness Chief, the laboratory refugee, being the brave one of the group. The tears started to roll…but for a great reason again. I hadn't done so much "happy crying" in my entire life.

The boys definitely take over the property when they are there, they jump out of the truck in the morning and we don't see them until lunch, then they rampage again until it's time to leave. Jager wasn't so keen on the entire day of nonstop activity. Bert would help him out of the truck in the morning; he would go exploring for an hour or so then come back and hang around with Bert. Chief had become quite independent but didn't quite have the stamina to keep up with Cowboy and Indian. Instead of running everywhere, Chief would jump up on to the seat of the Mule hoping someone was going to be driving somewhere. He had completely figured out where I kept the horses and that if I wasn't around, I was over at the barn with the horses. He trotted everywhere and was completely okay with being on his own or with Jager.

When The Fourth of July rolled around we were wondering how Chief would handle the firework situation. We were lucky enough to be staying in an apartment right on a beautiful, large lake. Every year on the 4th they put on a huge fireworks display that would last for about two hours. Poor Indian had become petrified of the fireworks and even when he heard gunshots at home would run, whining into the house and hide in the pillows on the bed. Chief had shown no signs of being afraid of the gunshots at home so both Bert and I assumed he would not be fazed by the fireworks.

We were about to find out what happens when you assume…We left the farm pretty late that night so the fireworks had started before we got to the apartment. We could hear them while we were driving in the truck and noticed that Indy had started to get nervous. Chief, on the other hand, was completely wiped out and curled up with Jager in the back seat. We unloaded everyone and headed inside, fed the puppies their dinner and settled in. To our surprise, Indian was fine. He curled up on the bed and went right to sleep amidst the booms, hisses, and bright lights. The longer the noises lasted, though, the more worried Chief became. He sat on the edge of the bed, had worried face on, panted like crazy and was very restless. We closed all the curtains and doors, turned on the TV and cuddled with him trying to get him to settle down. He didn't get worse but he certainly didn't get any better until almost one o'clock in the morning when the fireworks finally stopped. The moment the noise stopped, Chief passed out on the bed, took one huge breath and was off to sleep.

We couldn't even imagine what could have going through this poor guy's head for the last two hours. Was he having flashbacks to the lab? Did he think we had betrayed him in some way? Did he feel unsafe? We both felt a bit guilty that we hadn't prepared a little better for this situation, he had been doing so well and seemed so well adjusted, but in reality, he had only been out of a cage for a little over seven months. And while he had made great strides in that time, he still had so much to overcome. That morning, Chief made us both feel much better by being completely fine and happy and ready to go.

Chapter 59

The Show

About a week before the competition began, competitors started arriving and setting up "shop". The huge trade fair was being set up and there were new people, new dogs and new snacks to meet and eat. Cowboy and Indian were always a bit snarky for the first few days of the "invasion" they didn't like the idea of all these strangers on "their" property, and the fact that their freedom was curbed. Chief was happy as a clam to meet all these new dogs and it was so great to see him so full of confidence. He would walk up to new dogs and actually be a dog! He was a bit leery of the people around but not scared to death. So amazing. He was having such a blast. I would see him trotting over to where the trade fair was being set up looking for snacks, he would come by occasionally to say hi, but always seemed busy.

The competition began and I became consumed with the horses and the competition, the dogs were Bert's responsibility for the next few days which usually meant being in the truck because he was running around finishing things up. One afternoon he was able to let the boys out to run around while he was working. A couple of hours later I got a phone call from a friend telling me that she had found Jager wandering around and he didn't look good at all. He had been caught in the sprinkers so he was soaking wet and his hind end was not functioning and she was very worried about him. I told her where I was so she drove him over to me. I put him in my Mule and drove him back to the shop where Bert was working. I told him what had happened and he looked...sad. He carefully put him in the backseat of the truck and tucked him in. I had a pretty good feeling about what was going on in his head but I also knew he wasn't going to talk to me about it.

The horse show came and went and was a complete success. The dogs were so well behaved except when Indian jumped out of the truck and ran across one of the arenas while there was a horse jumping, luckily nothing happened as a result of that! The horses were fantastic and I had more fun than I had ever had at a show. Chief was a regular at the food vendor's area and always seemed to find something to eat! So much for his diet. What else could you ask for?

Chapter 60

Good Bye

It took only a day or so for the over 500 competitors to vacate the premises, and the property belonged to the beagles once again! It was time to get back to work cleaning everything up and I of course needed my number one weakness to help me through it…Cheetos! I kept my big bag rolled up in the glove box of the Mule I was using, needless to say, Chief always wanted to come with me, he only loved me for my snacks. Chief Cheetos was my co-pilot where ever I went.

It still concerned me to watch how frantic Chief would get about food, any food. He proved this to me one afternoon when we were finishing up for the day and I was unloading the Mule. He stayed up on the seat because it was hard for him to get up and down so he usually just stayed put until he was sure we weren't going anywhere again. While he was sitting there, I grabbed the bag of Cheeto's to put them in the truck and he completely panicked! Panic to the point that he just hurled his body off the Mule and face-planted right on the asphalt. He got up, shook, and ran up to me for a snack. I felt so bad as I looked at his bloody mouth and nose, checked him out and came to the conclusion that his wounds were only minor. I knew he wasn't hungry I only wished I could figure out how to make him realize it.

Cheeto Chief

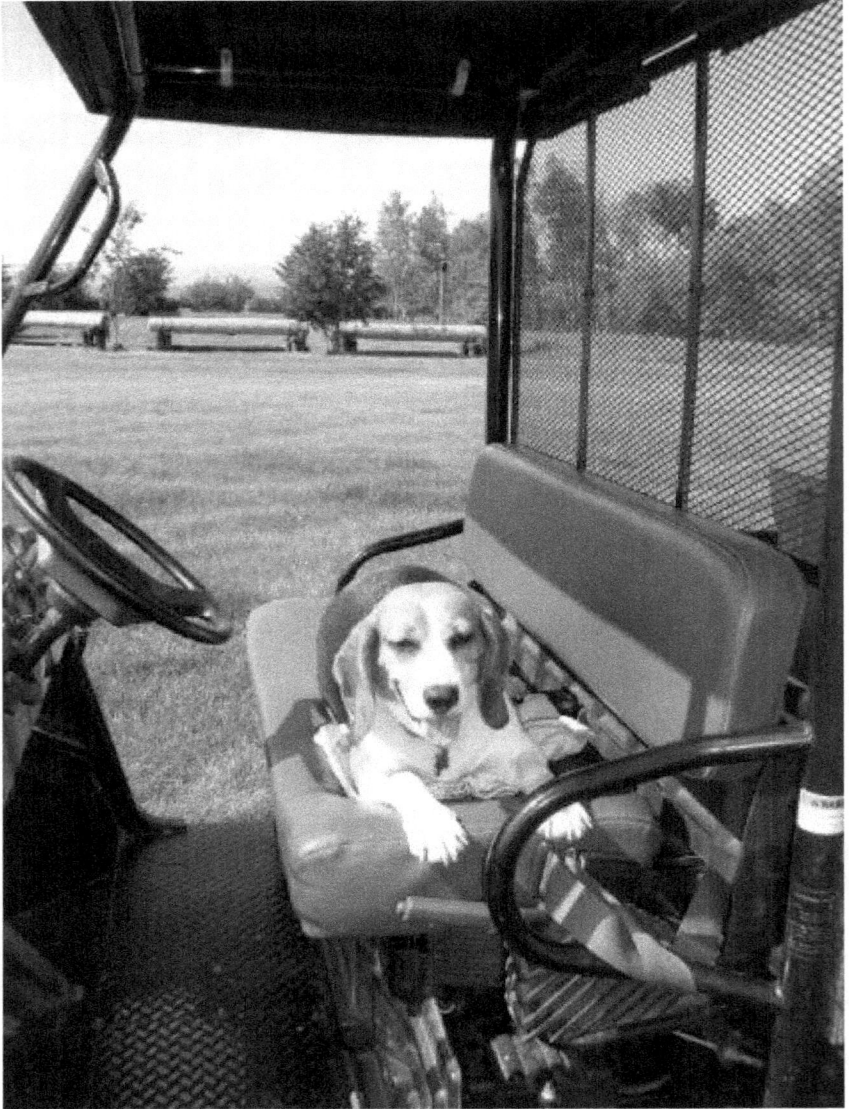

Chief stayed in the Mule as long as the Cheeto's did

We worked hard for about three days to get everything wrapped up. In that time Jager had some pretty bad days. His usual stomach of steel was a mess. He had a huge accident in the backseat of Bert's truck, in the cab of the piece of heavy equipment Bert was using to move the huge jumps around, and in the apartment where we were staying. On the Thursday after the show, Bert was busy working on a carving, which I was a bit confused about only because the show was over and work for next year wouldn't begin until spring. After watching for a while, I realized it was a headstone for Jager. He had fashioned a beautiful grave marker out of a cedar log and was in the process of carving words into the front of it. I knew at that point that today was the day; I left Bert alone to finish up without me hovering over him and went about my work.

It was lunchtime when Bert drove out to pick me up. He had Jager and Chief in the truck and simply said it was lunch time. We drove all around looking for Cowboy and Indian and soon discovered that they had caught the 600 acres are not enough disease. A "neighbor" had called Bert to let him know that he was holding on to Cowboy and had seen Indian running back towards the property line. Bert was becoming increasingly frustrated with this chase but I could tell it had nothing to do with the Beagles; it had everything to do with what would come when we finally caught up with them. After about forty minutes of driving around, we had four puppies in the truck. We headed to McDonald's to buy a 40 piece Chicken McNugget box for the "party".

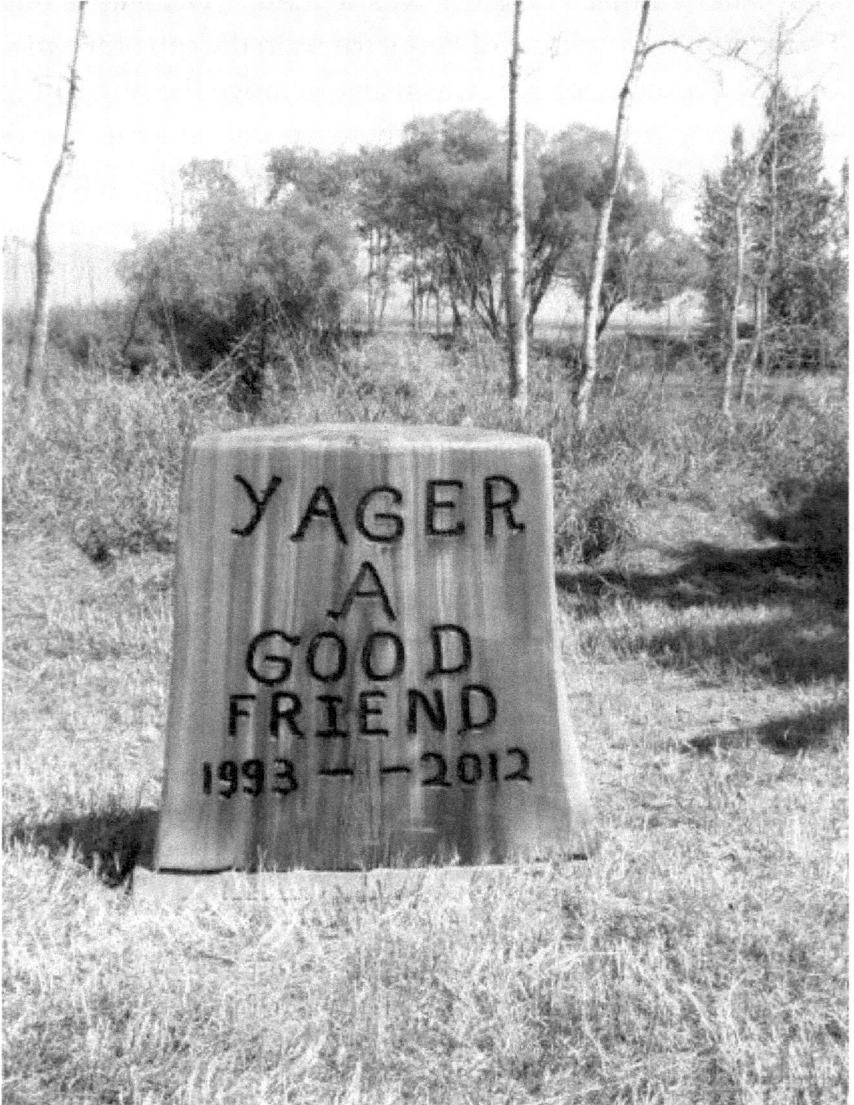

Bert and I never could agree on how to spell his name

Bert shared that we would go out to the "tree pond", one of Jager's favorite spots on the property, and have a Chicken McNugget party for the dogs, which was also one of Jager's favorite snacks. After which we would be there when Jager was put to sleep. I couldn't help but start to cry in the truck on the way back to the property, I hadn't known Jager nearly as long as Bert had but he had carved a very special place in my heart with his grouchy, growly entertaining personality. I also cried for Bert, 19 years, an incredibly long time to have a dog in your life, a dog that had been with him through thick and thin, a dog that everyone knew…it was Bert and Jager, Jager and Bert, pretty much inseparable. I couldn't even imagine what he must be feeling right now. All the dogs gathered around us and we shared the snacks with each one of them, soon the box was empty. Within twenty minutes, Jager fell asleep peacefully with a full tummy surrounded by those that loved him. Bert and I both cried as we buried him near the tree pond with his favorite quacking duck and his bed and the best view on the property.

I loved that Bert allowed me to be a part of this very difficult time and hoped I had been some kind of comfort for him. I think the beagles realized something was going on, maybe not what exactly but they knew that we were sad and stayed close for the rest of the day. Bert and I shared stories about Jager and talked about how quiet it was in the apartment that night not hearing him drink from the toilet or banging into things on his way out to bark at a noise no one else had heard. He had definitely left a big hole in our family.

Chapter 61

Time to Go

We packed up our belongings, the dogs belongings, stopping every time it was something of Jager's, all the horses' things and got ready for the long drive home. We stopped one more time by Jager's resting place, cried some more, talked about him, and then headed out. We had to decide who would have all three dogs, no more splitting two and two, so we decided they could ride with Bert. I followed Bert, who was hauling the new boat, while I hauled the horse trailer, we were quite the caravan. We pulled into our stop a little after midnight, unloaded the horses for the night and thought that sleeping on the boat would be a great idea.

We put all the dogs on board, climbed up and started rearranging things so we all had somewhere to sleep for a few hours. When I picked up a towel and a huge weight rolled out of it and hit the ground with a loud thud, poor Chief took a swan dive off the back of the boat. All I heard was a whimper and when I looked over the side of the boat, Chief was standing in the grass stone still. I yelled to Bert to please check him out that he had just launched off the back of the boat. He poked and prodded, squeezed and smooshed and told me he seemed fine. So, maybe staying on the boat was not a good idea. We loaded up the truck and headed to the nearest motel.

Chief still hadn't become comfortable with the whole motel idea. He never really relaxed while we were there and stayed up most of the night pacing and going from the bed to the couch and back again. The few hours of sleep we tried to get never really happened so we just packed up and headed out. We had about twelve hours left of the drive and by this point in the trip, just wanted to get home. It was, unfortunately, ridiculously hot on the rest of the trip home which made the twelve hours seem an awful lot longer. We went from the beautiful, green mountains of Montana to the flat, brown deserts of California. I always went through a bit of withdrawal after spending time in such a beautiful area, however, when we pulled into our driveway, heard Norman and Mo whinnying and saw them running around the pasture I was so glad to be home. The beagles knew we were home and had started reacting about an hour away from the house. We all piled out of our trucks, put the horses away, went in and went to bed. It still seemed so strange not to have Jager running around with us and snuggling into his bed when we got into ours. This was definitely going to take some getting used to but it was so nice to be home.

Chapter 62

The Dentist

Bert only had a few days to be home before he had to fly off to Michigan for the next big show. I would be joining him in about three weeks to work with him and the three dogs would be left home with mom for about two weeks. She was not pleased…and the puppies would not be either.

Until then, we went on trail rides and walks in the heat of the high desert summer. Chief was still not a fan of the hot weather and all three boys were happy with quiet days after their month long Montana adventure. I took this quiet time opportunity to take a close look in Chief's mouth. Not only was his breath still unbearable but he had two teeth that were so loose I couldn't believe they hadn't fallen out yet. His gums were black in some spots and if I pushed on them puss would come out right above the tooth. I had to do something. I knew all the beagles that came from Spain had gotten their teeth cleaned when they got here, but this was going to take more than a cleaning.

I found the number of a canine dental specialist that was nearby and called for an appointment. We headed down and I wondered how Chief would react to the sights and smells of a new vet's office. We walked in to the waiting room and as soon as we went through the door, Chief went into "the mode". He lost all expression, his head and tail went down,

The Dentist's Chair

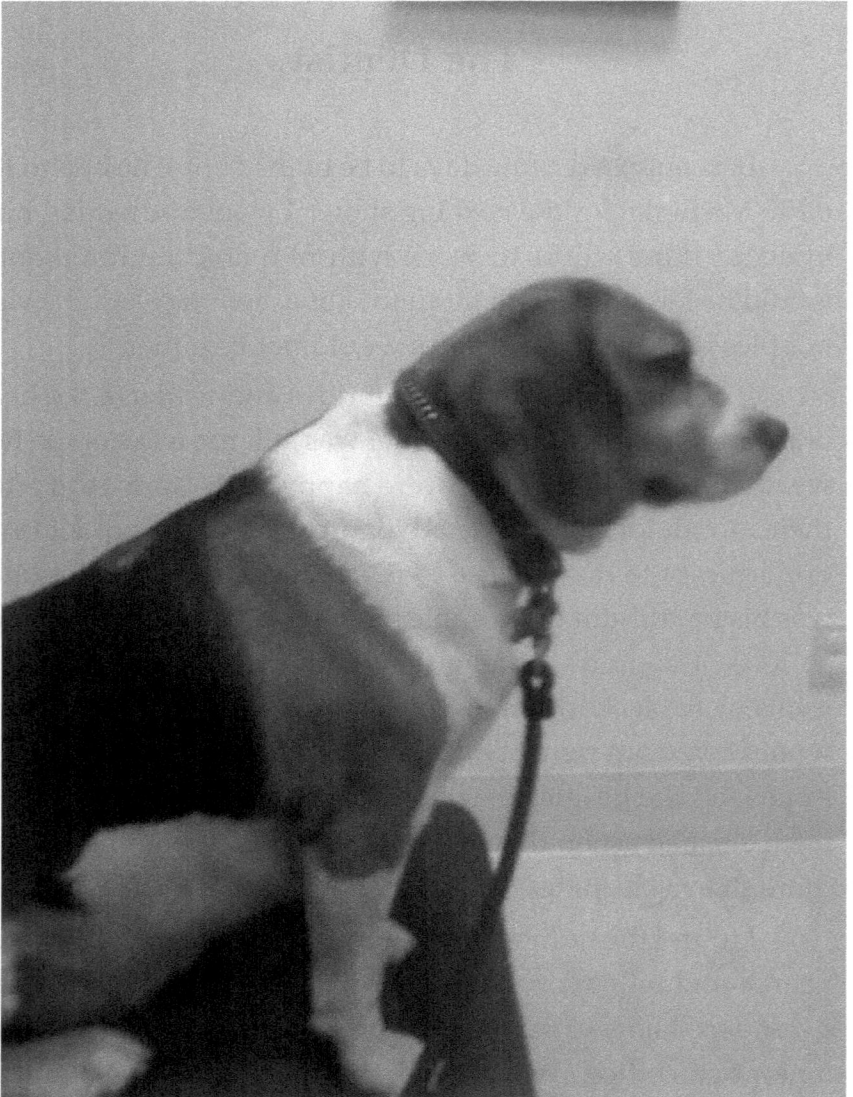

Chief just wanted it all to be over and sat so still

and he just seemed to say, "Just do it and get it over with." I felt so bad for making him go through this but I knew it was for his own good, I only wish he knew it too. We went into the examination to wait for the vet to come in. While we waited Chief jumped up on to the chair next to me and just sat there and waited with me. When the vet came in to the room to examine him, he stayed on the chair like that was where he was supposed to be and let the vet look in his mouth.

I had to take a picture with my phone and send it to Bert because it was so funny to see Chief just sitting in the chair and the vet looking at him. After the examination…the bad news! Chief was going to need some pretty major dental surgery to repair and eliminate the problems he had going on inside his mouth. The vet told me it wasn't the worst he had ever seen, but it was definitely very serious. About three thousand dollars' worth of surgery. I was floored. I knew Bert would not be impressed either. Chief was going to have to go in for blood work, a chest x-ray, x-rays of his mouth, and finally the actual surgery. I set the surgery up for the end of September hoping that would be enough time to scrape the money together.

Sure enough, when I spoke with Bert that night…he was not amused. We talked it over and I let him know how important it was to get this done. I told him what the dentist had said, how loose the two teeth were, and how many other problems can accompany a bad mouth. We did, however, share a laugh about Chief's eating habits; if this was how he ate when his teeth were rotting out of his head…what was it going to be like when his mouth was feeling good?

Chapter 63

Michigan

The three weeks at home flew by and I was off to Michigan to work with Bert at another horse show. The puppies could not have made it any harder to leave. I decided they should add sad Beagle faces to the "cruel and unusual punishment "list. I was in tears all the way to the airport. I was also feeling a bit guilty about leaving my mom with the three dogs as well as the four horses for such a long time.

The first morning I was in Michigan I received a picture on my phone from my vet. Norman had practically ripped his ear off somehow and my mom had to have the vet out first thing in the morning. Luckily she was able to stitch him all back together and he would be just fine. Unfortunately, it was another item on my mom's list of things to take care of. I was hoping this was not a sign of how things were going to go while we were gone.

To my surprise and sheer delight, the rest of the trip went without a hitch. My mom would go over and watch TV with the dogs for a few hours in the evening so they wouldn't be lonely. During the day they would stay outside with her while she was busy doing one thing or another or they would camp outside her door while she was inside, hoping for some kind of snack. The horses behaved themselves and Norman's ear was healing nicely.

I came home, once again, to squealing, licking, jumping, baying, and general craziness. It was great. I was so happy to be home and Bert would be there in a few days for some well -earned time off until the next big job. I noticed something in Chief over the next few days that I had never noticed before...I think he was pouting. He missed Bert, although he was happy I was there, he just didn't seem like his normal happy self. The moment Bert came through the door Chief was back in full form. I loved that Bert was really becoming attached to Chief and vice versa, I think their relationship made the fact that Jager was no longer there just a little bit easier on him.

Chapter 64

Surgery

Wow! September was here. Chief had been with us for nine months and, I must say, was doing ridiculously well. He loved going to work with Bert and was always the first one up and ready to go. He had become a trail ride pro and had more stamina every day. All three dogs were getting along and would sleep together on the couch or the bed together every night. Chief's waist line had continued to grow even with all of the exercise he had been getting and I was worried that once he had his mouth worked on it would just get worse.

I was hoping to save some money on the surgery by having the chest x-ray and the blood work done by our local vet. I had Bert take Chief in because it always made me feel like the "bad guy" to bring the dogs in for things. A few minutes into the appointment Bert called and asked if I could meet him at the vet's office. I, of course, started to panic in the split second it took him to say that Doc wanted to get the full story on why we were doing what we were doing. I took a deep breath made sure there was nothing wrong and headed over to the office.

When I arrived in the exam room, Doc already had that "Kris, Kris, Kris…" expression on his face, along with the head nodding. I explained the entire trip to the specialist, showed him the itemized list of what would be done, and then I showed him the estimate. Doc just about fell over in his chair. He went on to tell Bert and me that yes, even though what was going on in Chief's mouth was fairly advanced; it was not three thousand dollars advanced. He told us that Chief would need to have some teeth extracted and an aggressive cleaning done, and that he could make it cost three thousand dollars but that it only really needed to cost about three hundred dollars. Bert and I looked at each other, gave sighs of relief and booked the appointment for the next day.

Again, I had Bert drop him off first thing in the morning, so I could pick him up and look like the hero that was saving him from the horrible vet's office. I felt bad because the appointment happened to be on his birthday and because our animals are our children...I celebrate birthdays. We have dog parties with doggie ice cream, hot dog treats and new toys for the lucky boy. I know Chief couldn't have cared less what day he was getting his teeth yanked out but I did. It being his first birthday as a free beagle (which would soon turn into "freegle") and his first birthday with us, I had wanted to make it a special one. He had waited this long...I suppose he could wait one more day.

When I finally got to pick him up, I discovered that he had not two teeth pulled out, but ten. I did learn something new...dogs have forty four teeth so losing ten was not that bad. Chiefers was so happy to see me that he ran down the short hallway and just about knocked me over. Along with the bottle of antibiotics, Doc handed me a prescription for some diet dog food. What was he trying to say? He told me to give the antibiotics until they were gone and to use the prescription...Chief was much too heavy and this stuff was the only food that would work without leaving him hungry. As I was heaving Chiefopatamus into my truck, I agreed with Doc, we would start this diet as soon as possible. Well, after his birthday treats of course.

When we got home I noticed that the sides of Chief's mouth now sort of sunk in a bit, no teeth to hold it out any longer. He looked like one of those old southern men that forgot to put his teeth in. New nick name Chief Gummer. We went on with the party as planned, he ate his birthday hot dog, wasn't too sure what to make of the ice cream, gummed his new toy for a moment before Indian stole it from him, and actually let me put the ceremonial "SpongeBob" birthday hat on for pictures. He was such a good sport through all of this silliness. Both Bert and I hugged on him a great deal for the rest of the evening, so happy he was with us and so happy we were the ones to celebrate his first birthday as a freegle.

Within only a few days of starting the antibiotics, I could see a marked difference in Chief's energy level, general happiness and breath. It was another of those moments when I paused to think about how much his mouth must have been bothering him and the pain he was enduring all of this time due to the infection and rotten teeth. I loved to get in his face and snuggle before his procedure but now it was wonderful. Although he hadn't actually licked me yet the breath made it a much more attractive idea.

Chapter 65

Room for One More

October had arrived and with it another huge local horse show. Bert would be home for a while to work, Jay would be joining us for a few weeks and we would also have another visitor from England staying with us to help Bert. We were both curious to see if Chief would remember Jay and how he would react to having another male in the house. Luckily, he would meet them while he was at the show grounds, out and about, which worked great the first time he met Jay. When they all came home, Bert said his meeting with Richard and Jay was very successful and went off with no problems. Chief didn't seem to mind at all about meeting new people and his confidence was overwhelming.

Trying to fit everyone in the "dining/family room" was another story. Jay has his "chair" when he's in town, I usually sit on the floor, and Bert sits in his chair, this arrangement usually left the couch open for the three Beagles. However, for the next week, we had one more visitor, where would we put him? Luckily, Indian made had a habit of making himself very small at the very end of the couch on his pillow and Richard was a very understanding guest who sat on the floor with me or borrowed a small corner of the couch for meals and cocktails. The only time Chief reacted to either of them was first thing in the mornings when he would catch sight of either of them in the hallway and in the evenings...so basically anytime they were all in the house together. It took

Richard a few treats and sometime sitting on the floor for Chief to warm up to him but after just a few days he was fine with both of them.

The dogs loved it when Bert was home and were already at the truck door every morning to go to work. It was so funny to watch the truck pulling out of the driveway with three human heads across the front seat and three canine heads across the backseat. The boys were working long days and I was competing with two horses, so when the show began and the dogs were no longer allowed to go, the sad faces were back. Four days of trying to sneak out without seeing those faces was not easy! Four days of trying to get out of the house, down the driveway and out of the gate before the "herd" realized someone was leaving was another challenge all together. It ended up being another successful horse show for the both of us and the end of the season. Bert would have a short amount of time off before he was off again to work at many different venues. It was always nice to have the house guests gone, the horses on vacation, and just some time to snuggle with the beagles back in there

Chapter 66

One Year

November brought with it the one year anniversary of the "Spanish 40". We got an email inviting us to the celebration that would be held at a house in Los Angeles on November twenty fifth (the actual date was the twenty third but that was the day after Thanksgiving). All I could think of was how horrible the drive had been when we first went to meet Chief but it had been so worth it, I really thought it would be worth it this time as well. The Beagle Freedom Project had put on so many different functions throughout the year that I hadn't been able to attend for one reason or another and I wanted to make sure I was able to get to this one.

We had a wonderful Thanksgiving Holiday with the family, Chief's first one as a freegle. He had no problem deciding he loved turkey, gravy, mashed potatoes, and all the "fixins". We all went off our diets for this meal. All the dogs came out and played horse shoes with us and sometimes decided to stand right in the way of the whole game. We ate over at my mom's house so we were serenaded by the three Beagles for the majority of the meal, until we went back over to our house for dessert. All three puppies were crashed out on the couch in a turkey coma by the second helping of pie.

We reveled in the idea that Chief was here and wondered what he would have been going through at this time last year. He and the rest of the Spanish 40 would have been flying out the next day and we could only imagine the hustle and bustle that had to have been going on in Barcelona and here in LA as well, at this time last year. We talked about the story that Shannon had told us about the rescue and the days leading up to and following it; it was still almost unbelievable.

Chapter 67

Anniversary Party

I talked my friend Regina into taking the trip to Los Angeles with me. At least it wasn't Montana and we would only have one puppy, not a herd of horses and an entire pack of beagles. We left nice and early and the other guys were not at all impressed that they had to stay home alone while the new guy got to go. I had no idea what to expect and didn't think it would be a good idea just to invite Cows and Indy to the party. Chief had turned into the seasoned traveler and just fell asleep in the back seat for the duration. After, close to three hours, we pulled into a cute little neighborhood and saw a big sign that said, "Spanish 40 Reunion" with balloons all over it. We were a bit early, but as we drove past the house to find a parking space Regina pointed to the various TV station news trucks parked along the road. I was so excited to be there, the one function I was able to attend was going to be the most gratifying and I couldn't wait to get in there. We parked my massive, dirty, farm truck on the tiny road next to all the nice shiny, clean city cars, put Chief's leash on and headed to the party.

We were welcomed in the driveway by a host of people I, unfortunately, didn't know. They were all so nice and excited about Chief and I being there, I knew right away they had to have been involved in the rescue a year ago. We were invited into one of the cutest backyards I have ever been in. Lots of grass, a big playhouse, a swing set, a beautiful pergola with couches underneath…a perfect place for 40 beagles to reunite. I literally ran into Shannon, we chatted for a while about what had been going on, but she was obviously very busy so we made ourselves at home in the yard. I let Chief off his leash and he took right off to explore.

It didn't take long for the rest of the "40" to start showing up. Most of the adopters seemed to be acquainted so not only was this a reunion for the dogs but the adopters as well. As the families came in, they would let their beagles off their leashes and watch the fun begin! The media was busy interviewing Shannon and some of the adopters as well as filming the incredible dog party that was going on. I loved watching Chief interact with the other dogs, he played occasionally but spent most of his time sniffing around and visiting the snack table! I met the couple that had fostered him and they could not believe how much he had changed. I think that was their polite way of saying how much weight he had gained. Most of the forty were tall and lanky, none of them were small like Indian, and I must say that Chief was probably the heaviest one there.

Shannon was finally able to get everyone's attention and asked that we get into a circle to share stories about the last year with our "freegles". Before we got started, I noticed a women whispering to Shannon about something that was obviously very painful as she had tears in her eyes as she was talking to her. When she moved away, Shannon quieted everyone down for what she said was a "sad and difficult announcement". She proceeded to share that one of the adopters needed to find a new home for her beagle named Cinco. After a year, poor Cinco had still not gotten over his fear of this woman's husband, it had gotten to the point where Cinco would go out on walks and refuse to come home, he wouldn't stay in the same room with him if she wasn't there and he ran around the house to get away from him.

Chief was more interested in the plants

On some occasions Cinco would allow himself to be pet and snuggled by her husband but for the majority of the time it was a no go. I was almost in tears listening to her story, as I was trying to pick from all the wonderful stories about Chief to share, this was what she brought with her to this reunion. Shannon made the mistake of asking one of the people that happened to be close to Cinco to pick him up so everyone could see him. Unfortunately, it was a man that made the move to pick the poor guy up and Cinco started to freak out the second he was lifted from the ground.

That was it. I got my phone out and sent a text to Bert, who was out of town working, telling him briefly the story about Cinco. It took some time for a response and it actually took me by surprise. He told me we could take him if no one else would. I watched Cinco interact with the other dogs for a while thinking he may not have the best social skills if he was still that afraid of men. Not the case. He was having so much fun playing with the other dogs; he was almost more social than Chief was. He was a lighter fawn color with white legs, some black on his back and neck he also had a white "Y" on the back of his neck. He was taller and more lanky than Chief and had brown "eye make-up" where all of our other guys' was black. After watching him for a bit, I walked around looking for Shannon. When I finally found her, I told her that Bert and I were possibly interested in helping out with the "Cinco situation".

She had a huge smile on her face as she led me to Cinco's mom and introduced us; she left us to our conversation. I asked some general questions about Cinco and then proceeded to explain to her about where we lived, all about Chief and the progress he had made in the year he had been with us, about Cowboy and Indian, and finally about Bert. I wanted to assure her that he was quiet, gentle, and ridiculously low key. She sounded very interested and thought it sounded like a really good match. We were obviously trust worthy...otherwise we wouldn't have been approved to bring Chief home. I think I overwhelmed her with my interest and I don't know if she was expecting to find someone so quickly. We chatted for a bit and I just couldn't help myself…"I can take him with me today if that would work for you". After I said it I felt like I had been too forward and I saw a look of almost panic come over her face. She wanted to speak with her husband before any decisions were made and excused herself to give him a call. I told Regina what was going on and she smiled, laughed, and just rolled her eyes.

I sent a text to Bert that said, "We got him!" I was excited but a bit scared at the same time. I had already introduced Chief into our home and Cows and Indy had been very welcoming. How would they feel when I brought another one home? What if Cinco couldn't get used to Bert either? My head was swimming in "what ifs" and I all of a sudden realized I was panicking as well! In the midst of my "swimming" my phone starting tweeting, letting me know I had a response from Bert…"I know" was all he said. He made me smile with his usual sarcastic response and I started to feel more confident with my decision.

After about ten minutes she came back to me with a look on her face that I can only describe as a mixture of happiness, sadness, relief, and panic. She told me that she and her husband decided they didn't want him to go with me that day because they wanted a chance to say god bye and also to let their daughter say goodbye. We set up a time in a week for them to bring Cinco out to the "ranch" and tried to coordinate it with Shannon so she could be a part of it. We hugged, we cried, we hugged some more and said our good byes. I rounded up Chief and Regina, who was on the phone with her mom about some super cute pit bull puppies that were there, gave Cinco a huge hug and headed out to the truck. Chief was exhausted and crashed into beagle coma as soon as he got in the truck. The drive home was all conversation about the "other new guy", how much fun Chief had had, all the great stories we heard and all the new people we had met.

That night I channel surfed through all the network news channels that had been at the reunion. When I finally found one that was showing the footage, I was so happy to see that the majority of what they had was the Beefers. They had the camera at ground level and showed him sniffing around the yard, the lens, and the snack table. Of course, the water works began again and I just cried as I sat and watched the footage from the reunion. I felt so gratified, happy, proud, and so many other emotions that I just sat still for a while and enjoyed it all, especially looking at all three of my boys snuggled up together on the couch.

Chapter 68

Cinco

The week flew by and the day of Cinco's arrival was finally here. I wanted to get my horses ridden before they came so I would have the entire day to spend with him. I also wanted to get the boys out for a good long run on the trail so they would be nice and mellow when he arrived. My timing was perfect, right as I arrived home with all three dogs, our "puppy to be" and his family pulled on to the property. My mom came out when they arrived to meet everyone and keep everyone entertained while I put Homes away. Cinco's family met Cows, Indy, and Chief and I could see Cinco in the car just waiting to come out and meet everyone too. They seemed a bit unsure how to proceed so I just told them to let him out and see what happened. My experience up to this point with these three crazy beagles was to let it go and they would work it out on their own.

The door was opened and history was made. Cinco jumped out of the car and everyone ran to meet him. Tails were wagging, circles were being made, butts were being sniffed, but most importantly a new member of the family was being welcomed. Indian took the job of being "Welcome Wagon" and jumped into Cinco's car, nosed around a bit, grabbed Cinco's favorite toy they had brought with him and took off with it. Needless to say…it hasn't been seen since! It didn't take long for all four of them to take off in all different directions at all different speeds. Cinco was overwhelmed by all the smells, sights, new buddies, huge animals, new people and space but seemed to be loving it! I showed everyone into the house to share Cinco's new living arrangements with his family while all the dogs came in. Once again...Cowboy tried to guard all of the toys by barking and running from toy to toy. It truly looked like Indian was showing Cinco around the house, through the kitchen into the living room, into the bedroom and back out again. Chief was still very preoccupied with the kitchen so if anyone was in there, he usually was too. I assured Cinco's family he would be taken care of to the point of being spoiled, that I would keep them posted on his progress, and that we were over the top happy that he was joining our family.

They brought his big fluffy bed and a cute blanket that he slept with at home. I plunked it down on the floor by the wood stove and while we were chatting, he climbed right on it and sat in the middle of it looking like a king surveying his castle. I couldn't have asked for a more prepared family for the "hand off", not only did they bring a bag full of his goodies, they brought the half full bag of dry food he had been eating, the treats he liked, his harness, leash and cute little dog bone shaped poop baggie holder. I shared with them, of course, that poop baggies were not needed out here in the country.

When Cinco finally slowed down enough to say hi, I noticed he had a really serious looking scar on his hind leg, which I was told, was there when he had come home. The hair hadn't grown back over the scar tissue and it was right on his hock. Looking at it more closely it looked as though he had just about lost the entire lower part of his leg. It certainly didn't seem to impede his progress at all but it definitely put an absolutely hilarious hitch in his "get-a-long". Because he couldn't bend the joint completely, he had learned to compensate by swinging his whole leg out to the side. Cinco is a great looking beagle but, as Bert would say about horses, he's built a bit "down hill", which means his rear end is higher than his shoulders. He also has a chest that is wider than his rear end, so because of all his conformational quirks, watching this guy run made me laugh so hard I actually snorted. Add a slight downhill slope, a gentle breeze to make the ears fly and something worth running for and you have the recipe for one of the silliest yet happiest looking runs I had ever seen. His tongue seemed to be out everywhere he went and he had the biggest grin on his face. I also noticed one of his toes on his front paw was obviously broken at one time because when he stood certain ways it would twist at a strange angle. Although this "left over" from Cinco's lab stay didn't seem to affect him any longer either, it still broke my heart and made me shudder to think what had happened to this poor guy to give him such scars. Chief hadn't had any physical signs of blatant abuse but Cinco sure did. I was wondering what the emotional toll would be like, panic set in again, maybe this was too much for us to handle, maybe we couldn't "fix" him like I was hoping. Breathe, I told myself, he was already so happy, he had experience being a dog for a year…we got this.

After about an hour, goodbyes were said, some tears were shed and Cinco's first family was on their way. I found it pretty amazing how quickly the three dogs accepted Cinco into their little pack. There hadn't been any snarking or negativity or dominance between any of them. It was so reassuring. Although he had only been with us for a few hours...it was going really well. Just like I could always hear Chief speaking in his Antonio Banderas voice, I could now see, and hear, Cinco introducing himself to the boys in the voice of "The Most Interesting Man in the World", something like, "I don't always run around on my own but when I do...I run, like this!" However, we still had a few hurdles to jump over like feeding time, the doggie door, the horses, potty training yea or nay, bedtime, meeting Bert, I'm sure there was more. Okay maybe more than "a few" hurdles.

We also decided that Cinco needed a new name to go with his new life. We wanted something that sounded similar to Cinco but that fit in with our, I guess I should say my, "theme" of the west. We finally came up with Bronco. It was perfect; he did look like a bucking bronco when he ran around the property with his legs going in all different directions, his ears flapping, his tongue hanging out, and the huge smile on his face, okay maybe not like a horse but like an ecstatic freegle.

Chapter 69

Bronco

After a full day of running around and getting to know the property, it was time for dinner and the evening rituals. The eating arrangements had changed a bit since Jager had left us. Chief was now eating in Jager's spot, Cowboy and Indy both ate at different spots in the kitchen, so it seemed only fitting to find a spot for Bronco in the kitchen as well. They had all been getting along so well all day, I was hoping it would carry right on over into the evening.

Luckily, Bronco's "first mom" had brought the rest of his food with him; otherwise, as I would soon find out, he would have starved. If Chiefers was neurotic about food in an "I will eat anything and everything" kind of way, Bronco was neurotic about food in an "I will only eat this kind of food no matter what" kind of way. I wanted to wean him off the kind of food he came with and introduce him to the kind of food I was feeding Cows and Indy slowly. Bronco had other ideas! He would actually eat around the kibble that wasn't the kind he liked. There was never a problem with him eating the other guy's food or bothering them while they ate. He only ate his food and a few specific kinds of treats. It actually got to the point where he almost went two days without eating anything at all. New nickname Mr. Persnickety Pants…Finally, I caved. I found the strangest place in town

Bronco made himself comfortable right from the start. He sat in his bed and watched everything going on around him.

that carried the specific brand of dog food Bronco was obsessed with and changed all the guys over to that same brand. I had to give him a "taste test" on a spoon of the kind of wet food I was serving each night to see if it was a flavor he liked. If not he got a plain kibble dinner, if yes…he got a mouthful of wet food on the top.

The new eating arrangements were working out wonderfully so our next challenge was bed time. Bronco was going to have to find a place on the bed where he would fit…never mind if Bert or I would fit. Well, Bert was out of town working so it was only me that had to contort myself to fit in between all the boys. I climbed in bed, the three boys were in their places and we were just waiting for Bronco to figure out what he wanted to do. He made it up on the bed and decided the foot on my side was his. As he laid there I pet his big silky ears and noticed he too had tattoos in both ears like Chief. As if one laboratory experience wasn't bad enough, this meant he had been in two different labs.

Chief's one year anniversary was upon us and what a year it had been. We lost a treasured family member in Jager, but gained two new members in Chief and Bronco. It took me this long to realize my cute western themed names were also all names of professional sports teams, so not where I wanted that to go. We had watched Chief the thin, scared, timid, introverted, jumpy lab beagle turn into a vivacious, extroverted, chubby, independent dog. He had turned into "Mr. Personality" and made us laugh all the time. He was a solid pack member with Cowboy and Indian and had taken on the job of showing Bronco the ropes. His voracious appetite had not settled down yet and although he has lost quite a bit of weight, he is still on the heavy side.

I was guilty of living my life without much thought to where and how my "products" were made. However, now my eyes have been opened to the cruel and unnecessary world of animal testing. Watching Chief fight through the emotional trauma of five years in a cage and meeting and adopting Bronco with both physical and emotional scars was more than enough to make think twice about the things I was using around the house and for myself. I have since started using more and more cruelty free products, started to spread the word and raise money for the Beagle Freedom Project, and even started a social media page for Chief and Bronco to share their adventures and spread the word about other rescues and adoptions.

This is a story of how my husband and I rescued Chief from a horrible life, but he has given us so many priceless gifts in return, we look at it as a very fair trade. The resiliency and forgiveness he has shown in such a short period of time astounds us every day. There is a saying I have come across time after time, I have always liked it, but being a part of Chief and now Bronco's lives have made it a goal I try to attain everyday...

"My goal in life is to be as good of a person as my dog already thinks I am" –Author Unknown

Acknowledgements

Where Are They Now
During the one year reunion of the "Spanish 40" I was able to talk to most of the adopters to get some information on the beagles they had made family members. I asked each one the same six questions; the similarities were amazing and at times sad.

1. Original Number?
2. Movie Star Name?
3. New Name?
4. Any Medical Problems?
5. Most exciting/memorable milestone?
6. Any "left overs" from the past?

#1
Al Pacino
Uno

He had no health problems. Uno's greatest achievements were learning to bark and learning that treats are good! Uno still hates leashes and cowers from his harness. He is terrified of lap tops and will take off if he sees one.

#4
Ben Affleck
Chase

He had no health problems. Chase's greatest achievements were when he became sociable and outgoing and he loves the dog park. Chase is still easily frightened during walks on the leash. He is nervous around new people or in new situations. He becomes scared or "urban noises", mechanical noises still scare him and he prefers his crate if he is alone or scared.

#5
Harrison Ford
Cinco

He had blood in his urine and an enlarged prostate. When he was neutered, it eliminated the prostate problem. He has a bad scar on his hind leg and has a toe that turns out sideways sometimes. One of Cinco's greatest achievements happened when his new family arrived to meet him. Their 7 year old at the time sat on the lawn and #5 came over to her and put his head on her lap. She squealed, "Oh, please can we take him home?" She immediately reasoned that, "sometimes they pick you." Cinco's new dad threw up his arms and said, "Pack up his bed, we're taking him home."

The most memorable milestone was Cinco with his dad during the last week he was with us. It seemed that he knew he was going to transition to his forever home. His inhibitions and fear and anxiety that he had with him melted away and he would jump up on the couch next to him and lick his hand. Almost as if to say, "it's all good between us." It was a very comforting close to his year-long stay with us. Cinco was jumpy around men and scares at sudden movements and loud noises.

Bronco

For us, Bronco's greatest achievements were being calm and happy around Bert and learning to trail ride with the horses and the other dogs.
Bronco is still skittish in confined areas and hits the deck when any one raises their voice. He is easily startled by loud noises and quick movements.

#6
Matt Damon
Paco

He had very bad teeth, he had to have a few pulled, he also has a slight heart murmur.
Paco has become very friendly.
Paco stills howls when people are outside and is not a happy traveler.

#7
George Clooney
Chief

He had horrible teeth and had to have 10 pulled out; he also has a slight heart murmur and a small hernia on his belly.
Chief's greatest achievements were learning to bay, wagging his wonderful tail, and coming back to us when he was left to roam free.
Chief is still neurotic about his food and takes a while to warm up to new people.

#8
Tommy Lee Jones
Solomon

He had no health problems.
He was very scared and nervous when he came to us; he bonded with our other Beagle and with our daughter. He is very cooperative and likes to explore. He let us know our other dog had gotten out by barking at the door one afternoon.
Solomon is still very nervous and anxious. He likes to eat outside and the door must be closed before he will eat.

#9
Anthony Hopkins
Charlie (Chuckie)

He had severe dental problems; he now only has his front teeth. He also had facial trauma from being punched or kicked in the face.

Chuckie's greatest achievement was when he finally realized he was home and safe. He meets his mom after work by running faster than ever jumping on her and not getting off! Chuckie will still attack and bite if he is approached while lying down or if he is touched somewhere on his torso. But they are all learning to deal with this!

#10
Michael Cane
Willy

Willy experienced liver and spleen failure in January, he was in the "doggie ICU" and for four days was on deaths door. On day five he made a huge turn around and his organs began healing.

Willy's greatest achievements were playing with his new sister...they go nuts together. He goes on walks without freezing up and he is a great eater.

Willy still fears open spaces, sudden movements, and loud noises.

#12
Toby Maguire
Toby

He had no health problems.
Toby's biggest achievement was to finally stop shaking after ten days of being with his new family.
Toby still becomes afraid if someone is carrying something, he will bolt.

#13
Denzel Washington
Romeo

He had no health problems. However, he ate some things he wasn't supposed to and had to have surgery.
Romeo's greatest achievement was leaving the hearth after six weeks. He became best friends with his new sister, a Newfoundland named Grace. He also loves the dog park.
Romeo is still very scared of towels and spray bottles and he will not take food from any ones hands.

#16
Kirk Douglas
Kipper

He had no health problems.
Kipper's greatest achievement was walking on a leash without being afraid.
Kipper will always have his lab tattoo and suffers from separation anxiety. He prefers to go potty when he is out on a walk and will not go through the dog door to go outside.

#18
Sean Connery
Mack Thompson

He has an irregular heartbeat.
The most memorable moment was when the Beagle Freedom Project agreed to send him home with his new family.
Mack still does not like men and sometimes wakes up hyperventilating.

#19
Sylvester Stallone
Mateo

He had no health problems.
Mateo's most memorable achievement was when we were able to approach him with him "hitting the deck".
Mateo is still afraid of doorways and we are still working on potty training. He also becomes jumpy often.

#21
Lawrence Olivier
Archie

He had stomach problems when he came to us.
Archie's best achievement was the development of his personality. He loves his bed and feels like it is his safe place. He is no longer afraid of the leash and is great in the car.
Archie is still afraid of towels over his head, sudden movements and noises, and he does not like to be approached head on.

#22
Russell Crowe
Muppet

He had no medical problems.
Muppet did not bark, he was able to, he just didn't. One day he saw a squirrel on a walk and started barking and chased it up a tree.

Muppet will quite often, in the middle of the night, be sitting in bed just staring at the wall, when he is pet he will snap out of it and lay back down. When he is called he becomes apprehensive about coming and almost looks torn about whether or not he should come.

#23
Robert De Niro
Gadget

He had no health problems.
Gadget's most memorable achievement was the first time he played with a ball. Gadget still becomes fearful in certain situations and doesn't like loud sudden noises. If he is going through a doorway, it must be open.

#24
James Dean
Bauer

He had no health problems.
Bauer's greatest achievement was learning to play with their other dogs.
Bauer is still timid, shy, and scared.

#26
Hugh Grant
Avery – thing Bagel

He had no health problems.
Avery's biggest achievements were using a leash. He used to freeze with the leash on, now he will go and get it. He now looks for us when he feels worried instead of just running away.
Avery still suffers from separation anxiety.

#28
Nicholas Cage
Cooper

He has had chronic ear infections.
Cooper's greatest achievement was his bark. His family was told his vocal chords had been cut but after about eight months he let out the deepest, loudest bark on the way to the new dog park. Now, he barks all the time!
Cooper is still very suspicious of men and prefers to avoid them altogether. He is easily startled by sudden movements and noises.

#29
Pierce Bronson
Woodstock

He had no health problems.
Woodstock's greatest achievement was learning to climb the stairs.
Woodstock still growls when he is sleeping.

#30
Tom Hanks
Scout

He had no health problems. Latched on to Boomer (#39) they were adopted together.
Scout's greatest achievement was overcoming his fear of the house. He would stay in only one room and he is now all over the place. He also got away on a walk and was able to get home all on his own.
Scout is still afraid of people but he is getting better. He is also afraid of loud noises and sudden movements.

#32
Marlon Brando
Rico Suave

He had no major medical problems but very bad teeth.
Rico Sauvé's greatest accomplishment was his first tail wag and when he started moving around the house on his own.
Rico Suave shuts down completely during any type of procedures and is still jumpy about loud noises.

#33
Antonio Banderas
Walden (AKA Ol'Sorrowful Jones)

He had green rotting teeth and he was pumped up on steroids. Walden's greatest achievement was when he finally left the couch on his own. He sat on the couch for weeks and would have to be carried outside and then back inside many times a day. His milestone was when he finally did it on his own and went outside! He is now in and out and even using the doggie door. Walden is still very jumpy at noises and eats fabric and paper.

#36
Sydney Poitier
Freddie

He had some stomach problems.
Freddie's biggest accomplishment was when he first showed signs of affection. He would put his head in my lap. He didn't know how to give affection of get it but he laid his head in my lap with his butt up in the air.
His leftovers are is nervousness and skittishness around people.

#39
Morgan Freeman
Boomer

He had no health problems but was the most reluctant to come out of his crate. Latched on to Scout (#30) they were adopted together. Boomer's greatest achievement was learning to bay…all the time! Boomer still fears humans, loud noises and sudden movements.

#40
Jack Nicholson
Douglass

No medical problems.
For the first six days we had Douglass, he would not let us touch him. On the sixth day, he began letting us touch him and be around him. Douglass is still very fearful when he enters a room. He does not like going through doorways.

Although I was not able to get in touch with all forty of the "Spanish 40" adopters, all the Beagles are being well taken care of and are all overcoming the hurdles they must to become well-adjusted and happy "freegles".

www.ingramcontent.com/pod-product-compliance
Lightning Source LLC
Chambersburg PA
CBHW060737050426
42449CB00008B/1256